Level 1 • Part 1
Integrated Chinese
中文听说读写　中文聽説讀寫

CHARACTER WORKBOOK
Simplified and Traditional Characters

Third Edition

THIRD EDITION BY

Yuehua Liu and Tao-chung Yao
Nyan-Ping Bi, Liangyan Ge, Yaohua Shi

ORIGINAL EDITION BY

Tao-chung Yao and Yuehua Liu
Liangyan Ge, Yea-fen Chen, Nyan-Ping Bi,
Xiaojun Wang, Yaohua Shi

CHENG & TSUI COMPANY

Boston

26 25 24 23 22   11 12 13 14 15

Published by
Cheng & Tsui Company, Inc.
25 West Street
Boston, MA 02111-1213 USA
Fax (617) 426-3669
www.cheng-tsui.com
"Bringing Asia to the World"™

ISBN 978-0-88727-648-4

Cover Design: studioradia.com

Cover Photographs: Man with map © Getty Images; Shanghai skyline © David Pedre/iStockphoto; Building with masks © Wu Jie; Night market © Andrew Buko. Used by permission.

Interior Design: hiSoft

The *Integrated Chinese* series includes books, workbooks, character workbooks, audio products, multimedia products, teacher's resources, and more. Visit **www.cheng-tsui.com** for more information on the other components of *Integrated Chinese*.

Printed in the United States of America

CONTENTS

Preface

This completely revised and redesigned Character Workbook is meant to accompany the third edition of *Integrated Chinese (IC)*. It has been over ten years since the *IC* series came into existence in 1997. During these years, amid all the historical changes that took place in China and the rest of the world, the demand for Chinese language teaching/learning materials has grown dramatically. We are greatly encouraged by the fact that *IC* not only has been a widely used textbook at the college level all over the United States and beyond, but also has become increasingly popular for advanced language students in high schools. Based on user feedback, we have made numerous changes so that the Character Workbook can become an even more useful tool for students of Chinese.

Stressing the importance of learning a new character by its components

Learning a new character becomes much easier if the student can identify its components. The student should learn how to write the 40 radicals at the beginning of the Character Workbook in the correct stroke order first, because these 40 radicals will appear repeatedly in other characters later. If a new character contains a component already familiar to the student, the stroke order of that component will not be introduced again. However, we will show the stroke order of all new components as they appear when we introduce new characters. For example, when we introduce the character 孩 (hái, child) in Lesson 2, we do not show the stroke order for the radical 子 (zǐ, son) because 子 already appeared in the radical section. Therefore, we only display the stroke order for the other component 亥 (hài, the last of the Twelve Earthly Branches). For the same reason, when 亥 appears in the new character 刻 (kè, quarter of an hour) in Lesson 3, its stroke order is not displayed. When the student learns a new character, he or she can easily tell if a component in the character has appeared in previous lessons. If the stroke order for that component is not displayed, it means that the component is not new. The student should try to recall where he or she has seen it before. By doing so, the student can connect new characters with old ones and build up a character bank. We believe that learning by association will help the student memorize characters better.

Main features of the new Character Workbook

a. Both traditional and simplified characters are introduced
If a character appears in both traditional and simplified form, we show both to accommodate different learner needs.

b. Pinyin and English definition are clearly noted
We have moved the pinyin and the English definition above each character for easy recognition and review.

c. Radicals are highlighted

The radical of each character is highlighted. Knowing what radical group a character belongs to is essential when looking up that character in a traditional dictionary where the characters are arranged according to their radicals. To a certain extent, radicals can also help the student decipher the meaning of a character. For example, characters containing the radical 貝/贝 (bèi, shell), such as 貴/贵 (guì, expensive), and 貨/货 (huò, merchandise), are often associated with money or value. The student can group the characters sharing the same radical together and learn them by association.

d. Stroke order is prominently displayed

Another feature that we think is important is the numbering of each stroke in the order of its appearance. Each number is marked at the beginning of that particular stroke. We firmly believe that it is essential to write a character in the correct stroke order, and to know where each stroke begins and ends. To display the stroke order more prominently, we have moved the step-by-step character writing demonstration next to the main characters.

e. A "training wheel" is provided

We also provide grids with fine shaded lines inside to help the student better envision and balance their characters when practicing.

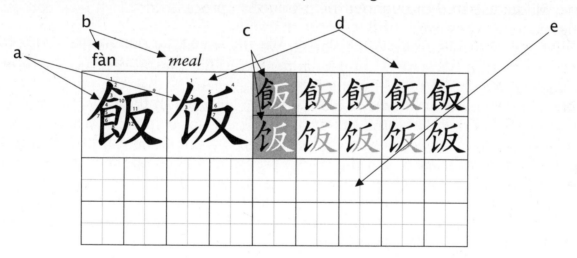

Other changes in the new edition

In order to focus on character recognition and acquisition, we decided not to include elements having to do with phonetic identification and phrase recognition.

To help the student look up characters more easily and to make the Character Workbook smaller and more portable, we decided to limit the indices to two, one arranged alphabetically by pinyin and the other by lesson. Additional appendices that are not directly linked to the practice of writing characters, such as the English-Chinese glossary, are available in the Textbook.

As in the textbook, low-frequency characters are indicated in gray in the Character Workbook.

The formation and radical of each character in this book are based on the *Modern Chinese Dictionary* (現代漢語詞典/现代汉语词典) published by the Commercial Press (商務印書館/商务印书馆). A total of 201 radicals appear in that dictionary, and in some cases the same character is listed under more than one radical. For the characters in this book that fall in that category, we provide two radicals in order to facilitate students' dictionary searches. The two radicals are presented in order from top to bottom (e.g., 名: 夕, 口), left to right (e.g., 功：工, 力), and large to small (e.g., 章: 音, 立; 麻: 麻, 广). Also following the *Modern Chinese Dictionary*, we have made adjustments with regard to variant forms: For example, 黃, 望, 綫, 麽 and 别 are presented as standard rather than 黄, 望, 線, 麼, and 別 respectively. Students, however, should be allowed to write the characters in their variant forms.

The changes that we made in the new version reflect the collective wishes of the users. We would like to take this opportunity to thank those who gave us feedback on how to improve the Character Workbook. We would like to acknowledge in particular Professor Hu Shuangbao of Beijing University and Professor Shi Dingguo of Beijing Language and Culture University, both of whom read the entire manuscript and offered invaluable comments and suggestions for revision. Ms. Laurel Damashek at Cheng & Tsui assisted throughout the production process.

We hope you find this new edition useful. We welcome your comments and feedback. Please report any typos or other errors to **editor@cheng-tsui.com.**

Radicals

rén   *person*

dāo   *knife*

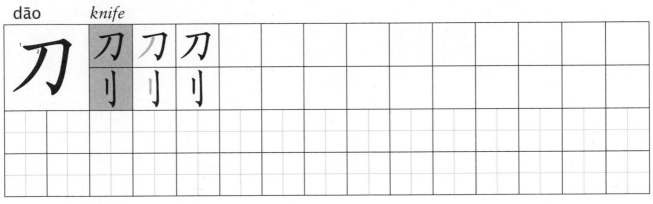

lì   *power*

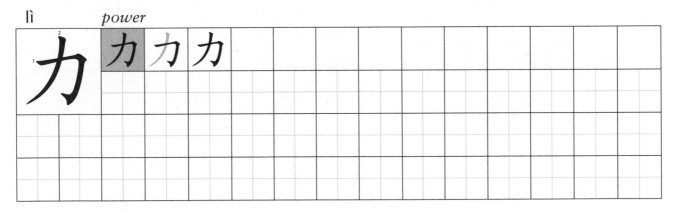

yòu   *right hand; again*

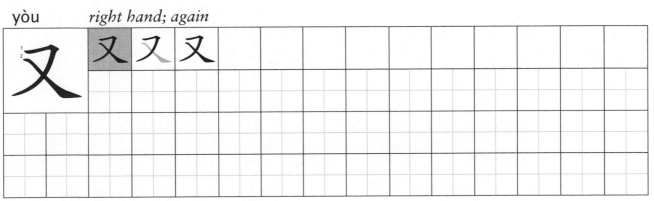

kǒu   *mouth*

wéi   *enclose*

tǔ   *earth*

xī   *sunset*

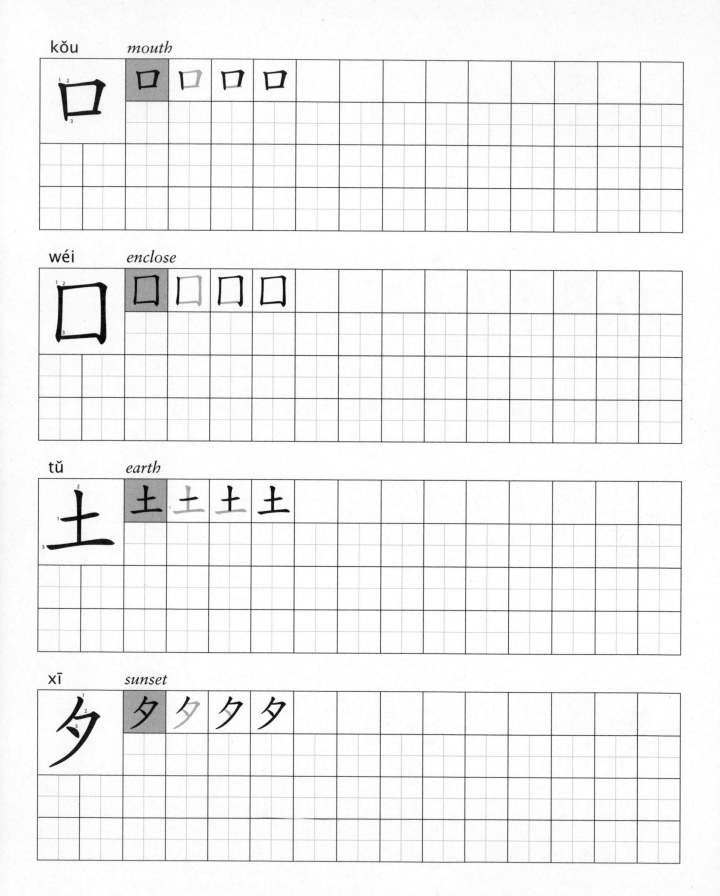

dà   *big*

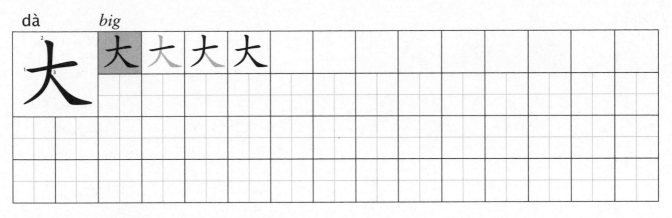

nǚ   *woman*

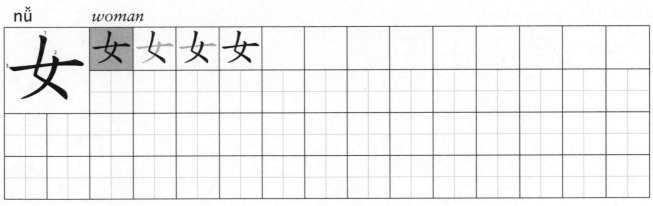

zǐ   *son*

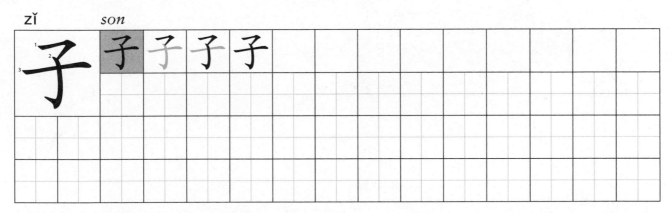

cùn   *inch*

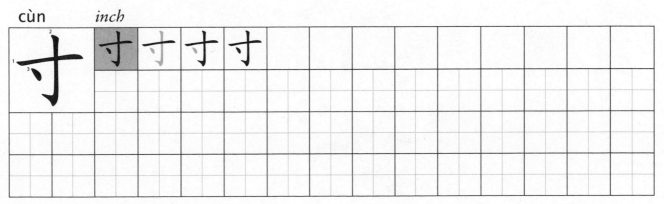

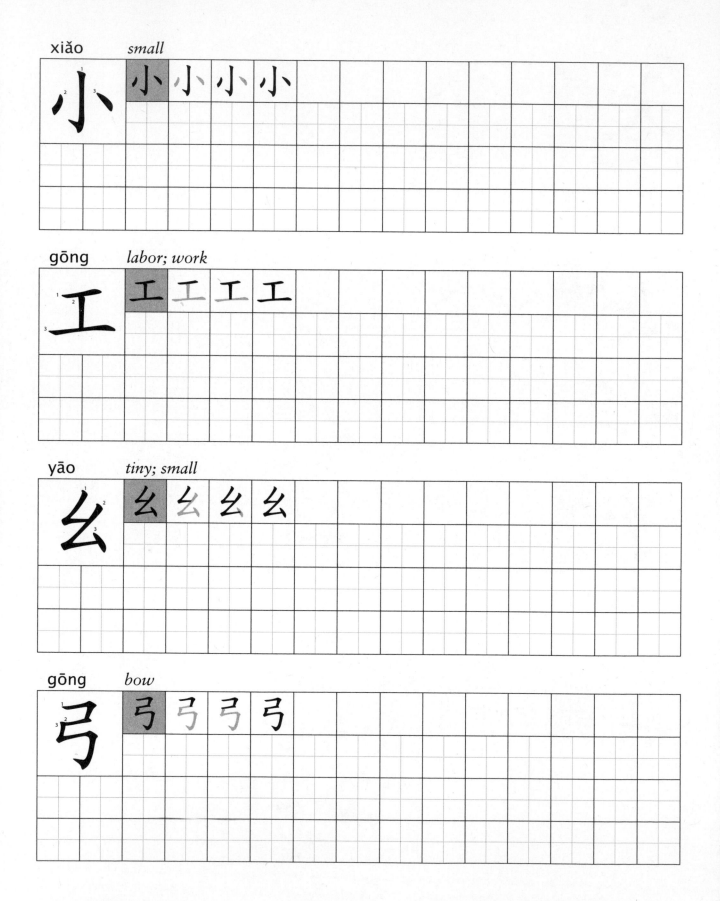

xiǎo   *small*

小

gōng   *labor; work*

工

yāo   *tiny; small*

幺

gōng   *bow*

弓

xīn   *heart*

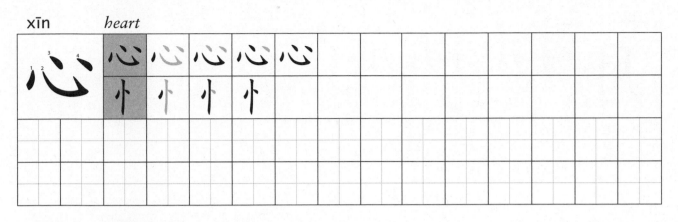

gē   *dagger-axe*

shǒu   *hand*

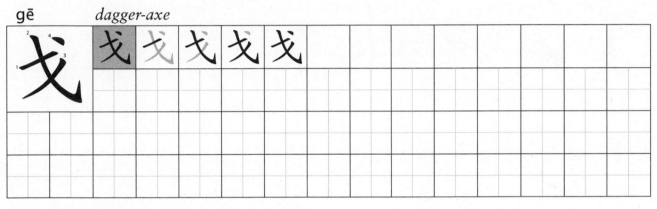

rì   *sun*

yuè   *moon*

mù   *wood*

shuǐ   *water*

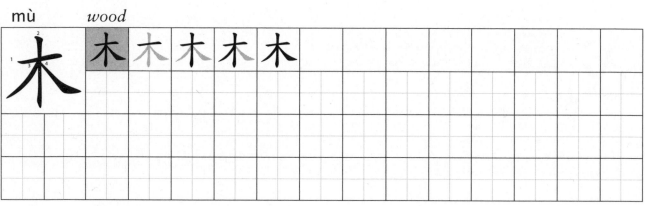

huǒ   *fire*

tián   *field*

田　田 田 田 田 田

mù   *eye*

目　目 目 目 目 目

shì   *show*

示　示 示 示 示 示
　　礻 礻 礻 礻

mì   *fine silk*

糸 糸 糸 糸 糸 糸 糸 糸

糸 糸 糸 糸 糸 糸 糸

纟 纟 纟 纟

ěr   *ear*

耳 耳 耳 耳 耳 耳 耳 耳

yī   *clothing*

衣 衣 衣 衣 衣 衣 衣 衣

礻 礻 礻 礻 礻 礻

yán   *speech*

言

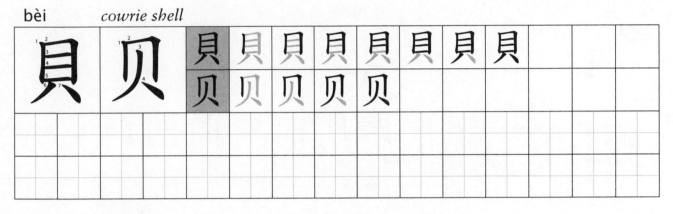

bèi   *cowrie shell*

貝　贝

zǒu   *walk*

走

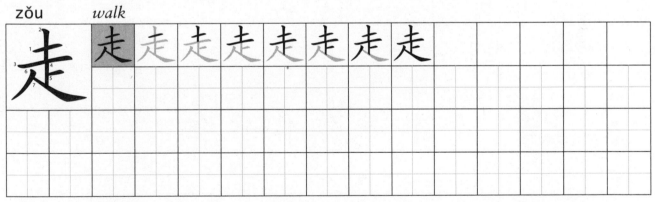

zú   *foot*

足

jīn   *gold*

金

mén   *door*

門   门

zhuī   *short-tailed bird*

隹

yǔ   *rain*

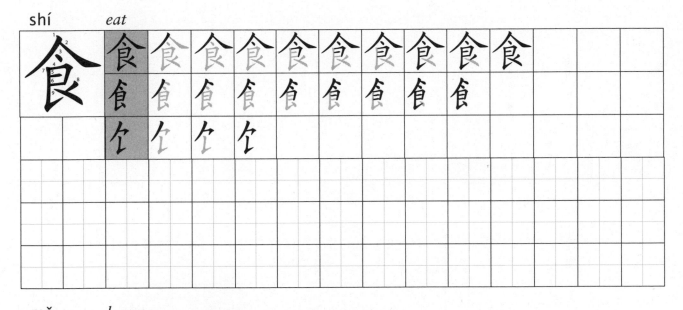

shí   *eat*

mǎ   *horse*

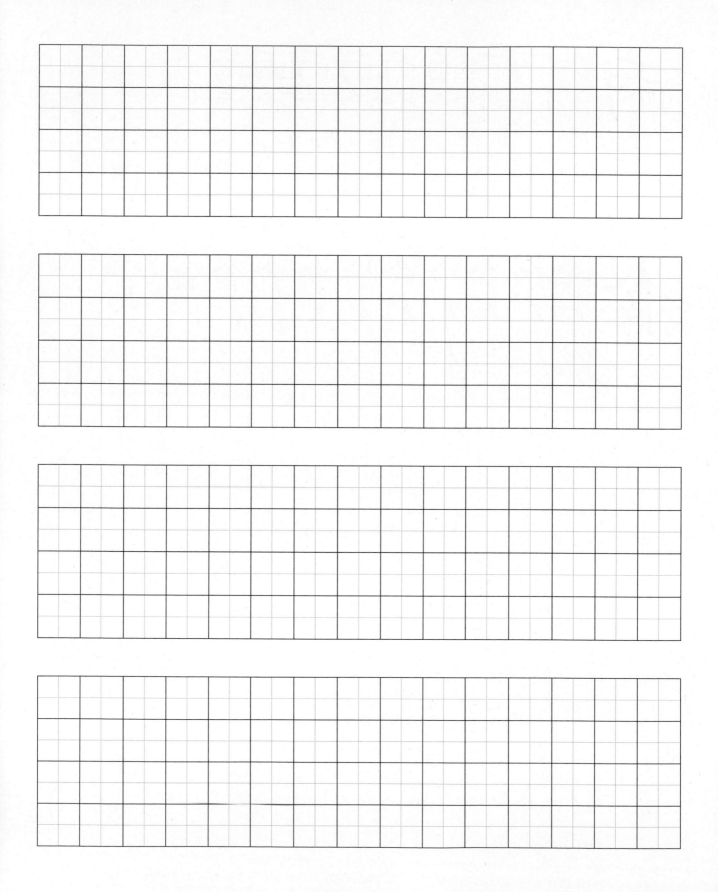

Numerals

yī *one*

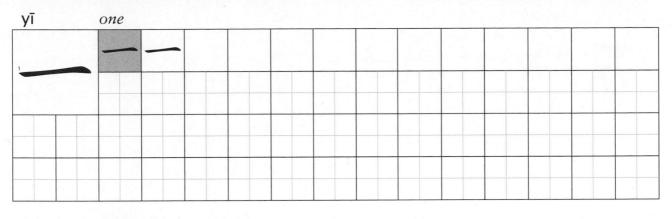

èr *two*

sān *three*

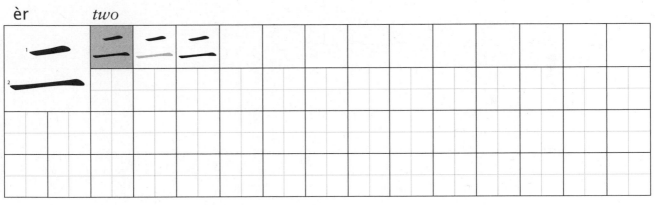

sì *four*

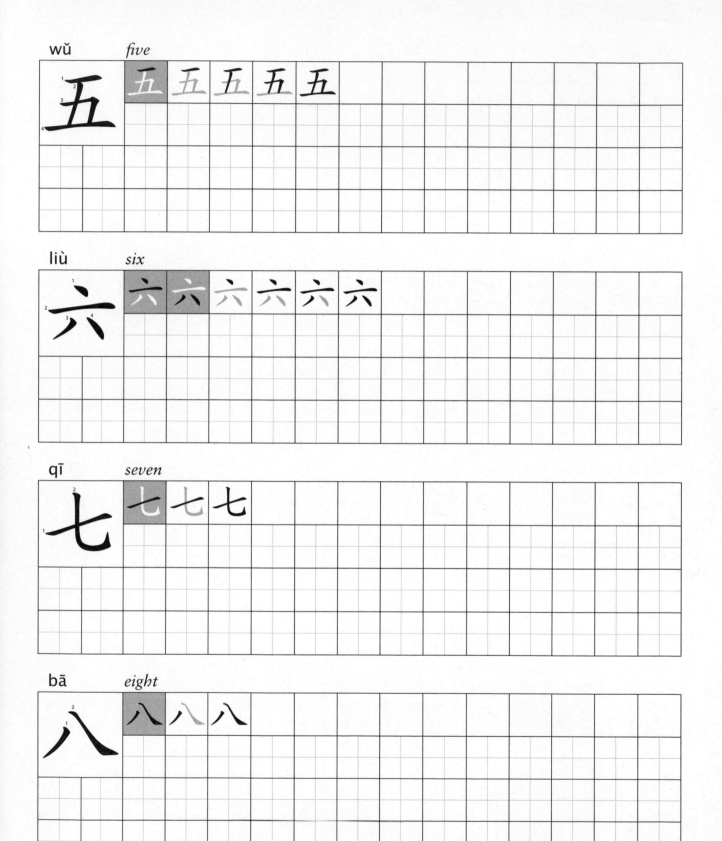

wǔ   *five*

liù   *six*

qī   *seven*

bā   *eight*

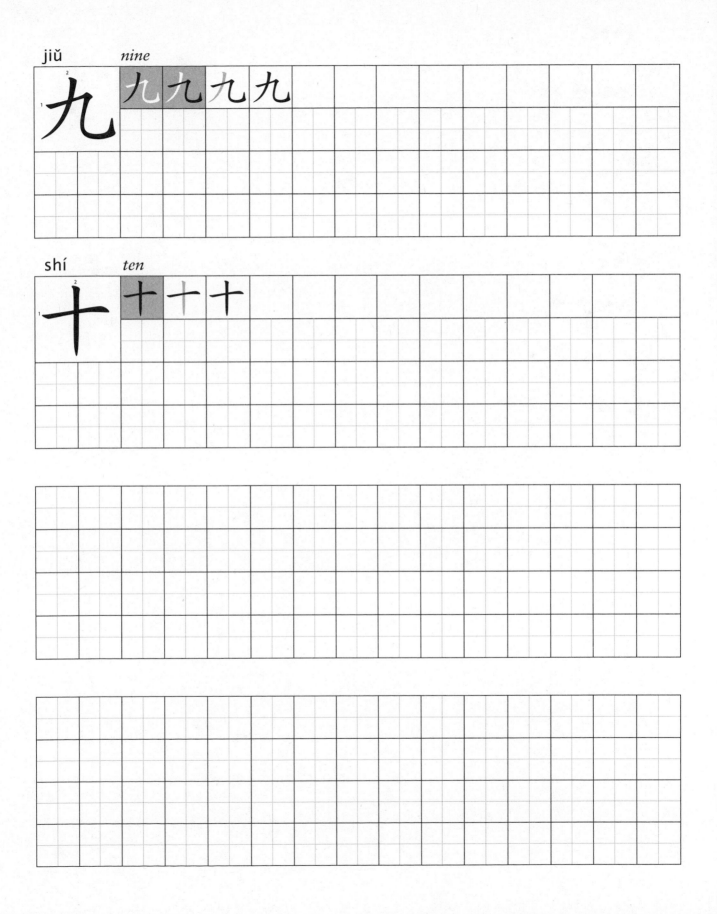

jiǔ *nine*

shí *ten*

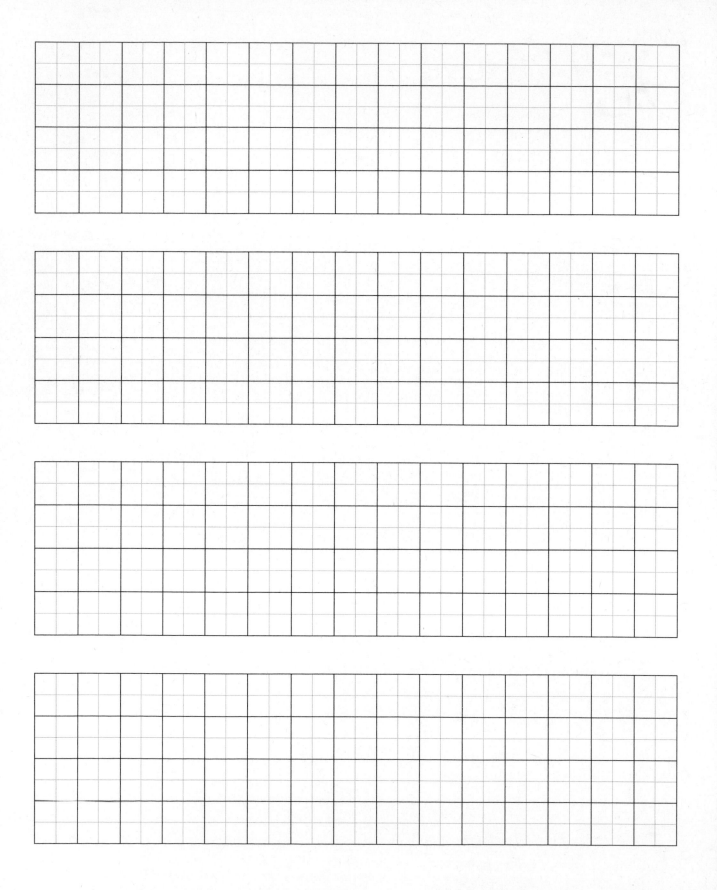

Dialogue I

nǐ   *you*

你 你你你你你

hǎo   *fine; good; OK; nice; it's settled*

好 好好好

qǐng   *please (polite form of request); to treat or to invite (somebody)*

請 请 请請請請請請請
请请请请请请请

wèn   *to ask (a question)*

問 问 問問問
问问问

guì   *honorable; expensive*

貴　贵

xìng   *(one's) surname is ...; to be surnamed; surname*

姓

wǒ   *I; me*

我

ne   *(question particle)*

呢

jiě　　　*older sister*

jiào　　　*to be called; to call*

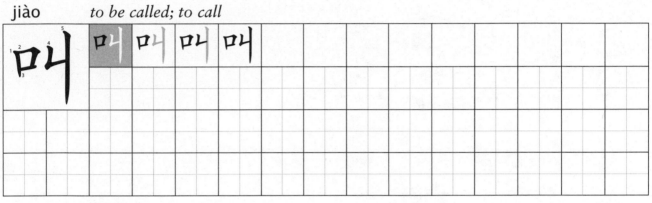

shén　　　*what*

什

me　　　*(question particle)*

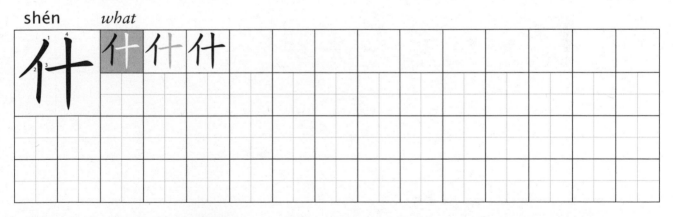

míng   *name*

zì   *character*

xiān   *first*

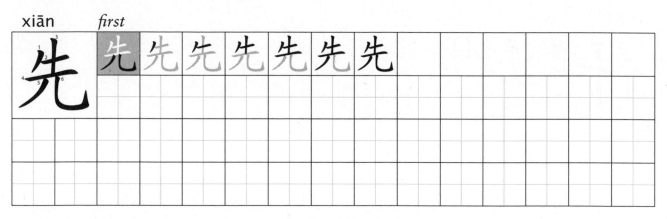

shēng   *birth; to be born*

生

Characters from Proper Nouns

lǐ   *(a surname); plum*

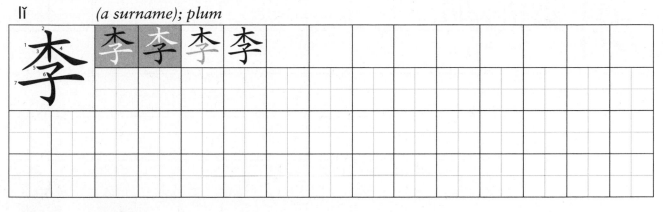

yǒu   *friend*

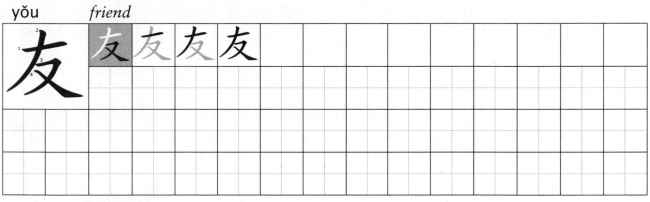

wáng   *(a surname); king*

王

péng *friend*

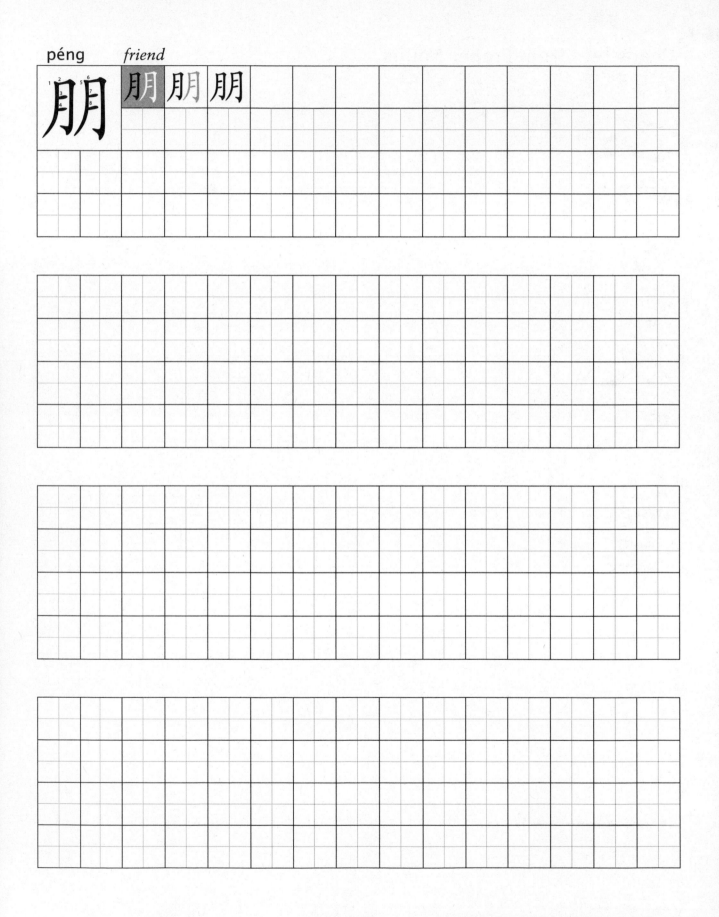

Dialogue II

shì   *to be*

是

是	是	是	是	是	是	是			

lǎo   *old*

老

老	老	老	老	老					

shī   *teacher*

師 师

師	師	師	師	師	師	師	師	師	師
师	师	师	师	师	师	师	师		

ma   *(question particle)*

嗎 吗

嗎	嗎	嗎							
吗	吗	吗							

bù   *not; no*

不 不 不 不 不 不

xué   *to study*

學 學 學 學 學 學 學 學 學 學 學
學 學 學 學
学 学 学 学 学 学 学

yě   *too; also*

也 也 也 也 也

rén   *people; person*

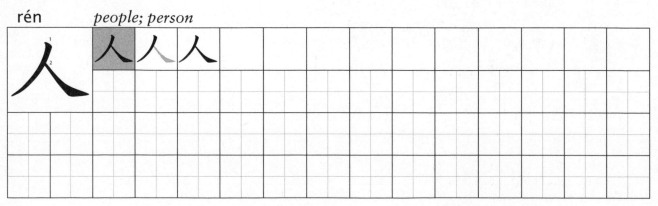

人 人 人 人

Characters from Proper Nouns

zhōng *center; middle*

中

guó *country; nation*

國 国

běi *north*

北

jīng   *capital city*

京

京 京 京 京 京

měi   *beautiful*

美

美 美 美 美 美 美 美 美

niǔ   *knob; button*

紐 纽

紐 紐 紐 紐 紐
纽 纽 纽 纽 纽

yuē   *agreement; appointment*

約 约

約 約 約 約 約
约 约 约 约 约

Dialogue I

nà   *that*

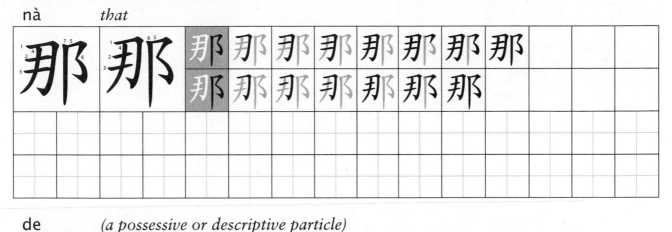

de   *(a possessive or descriptive particle)*

的

的 的 的

zhào   *photograph; to illuminate; to shine*

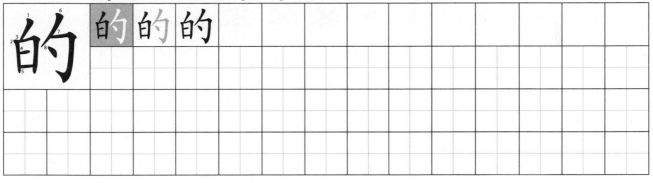

piàn   *flat, thin piece*

片

片 片 片 片 片

zhè *this*

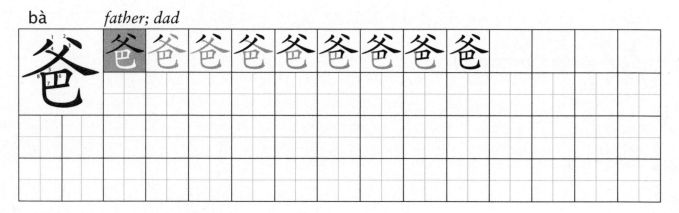

bà *father; dad*

mā *mother; mom*

gè/ge *(measure word for many common objects)*

hái   *child*

孩 孩 孩 孩 孩 孩 孩 孩

shéi   *who*

誰 谁 誰 誰 誰
         谁 谁 谁

tā   *she; her*

她 她 她 她

nán   *male*

男 男 男 男

dì   *younger brother*

tā   *he; him*

他他他

gē   *older brother*

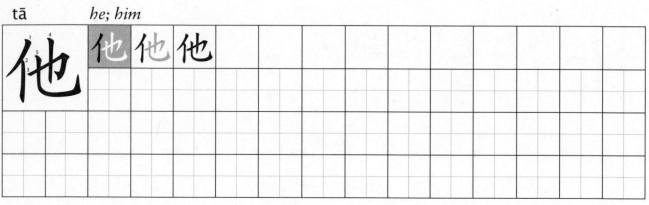

ér   *son; child*

兒儿

yǒu   *to have; to exist*

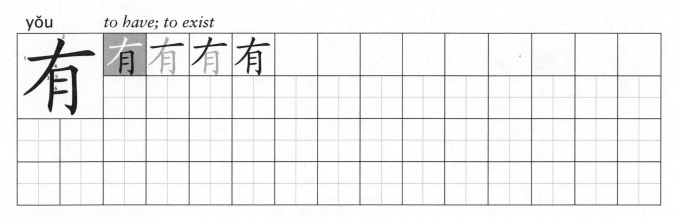

méi   *not*

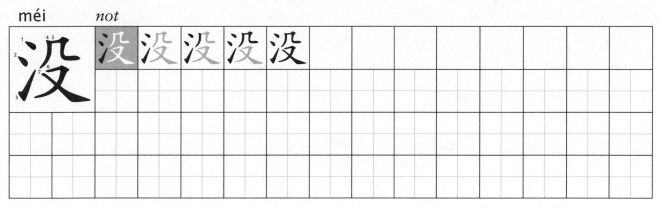

Characters from Proper Nouns

gāo   *(a surname); tall; high*

高高高高高高高

wén   *(written) language; script*

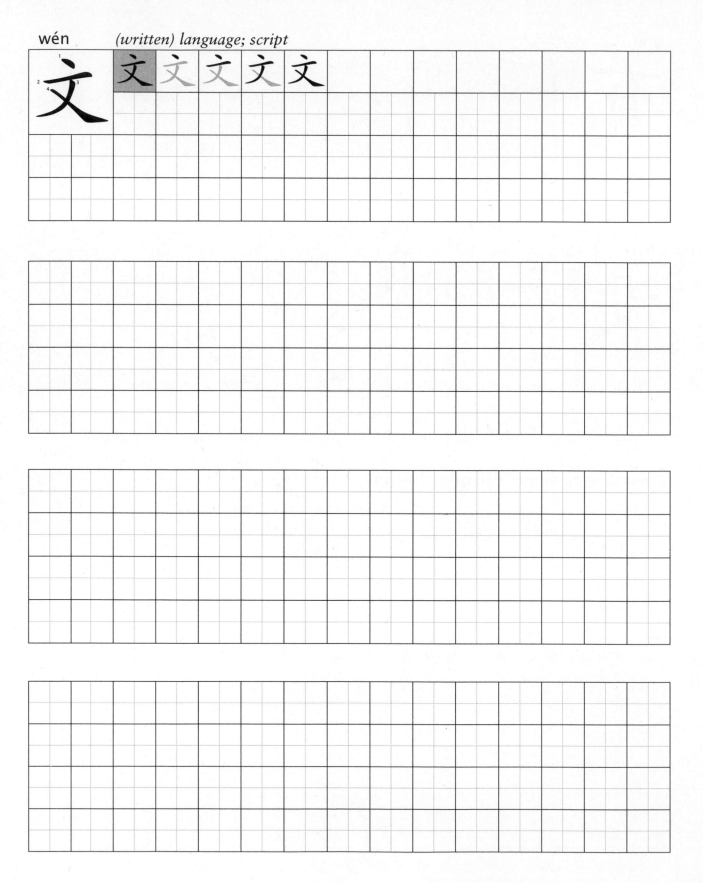

Dialogue II

jiā   *family; home*

家

家 家 家 家 家 家 家 家 家 家

jǐ   *how many; some; a few*

幾 几

幾 幾 幾 幾 幾 幾 幾 幾 幾

几 几 几

liǎng   *two; a couple of*

兩 两

两 两 两 两 两 两 两

两 两 两 两 两

mèi   *younger sister*

妹

妹 妹 妹 妹 妹 妹 妹

hé   *and*

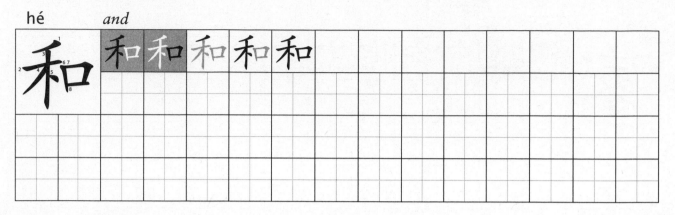

zuò   *to do*

zuò   *to work; to do*

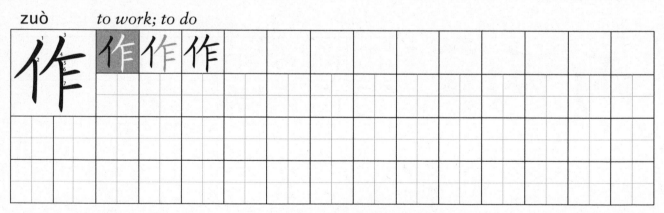

lǜ   *law; rule*

dōu   *both; all*

都 都 都 都 都 都 都 都 都
都 都 都 都 都 都

yī   *doctor; medicine*

醫 医 醫 醫 醫 醫 醫 醫 醫 醫 醫 醫 醫
醫 醫 醫 醫 醫
医 医 医 医 医 医 医 医

Characters from Proper Nouns

bái   *(a surname); white*

白 白 白 白

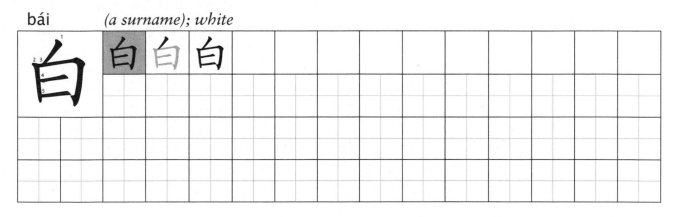

yīng   *flower; hero; England*

英 英 英 英 英 英 英 英 英 英 英
英 英 英 英 英 英 英 英 英

ài   *love; to love*

愛 愛 愛 愛 愛 愛 愛 愛 愛 愛 愛
爱 爱 爱 爱 爱 爱 爱 爱

Dialogue I

hào   *(measure word for a number in a series; day of the month)*

號 号 號 號 號 號 號 號 號 號 號 號
号 号 号 号

xīng   *star*

星 星 星 星

qī   *period (of time)*

期 期 期 期 期 期 期 期 期 期

tiān   *day*

天 天 天 天 天

jīn   *today; now*

nián   *year*

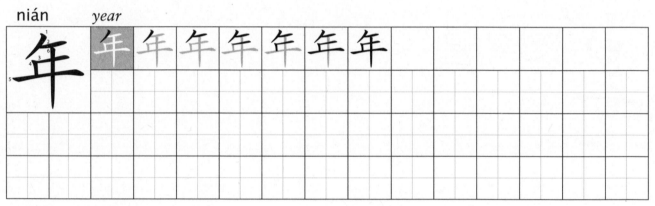

duō   *many/much; how many/much; to what extent*

suì   *year (of age)*

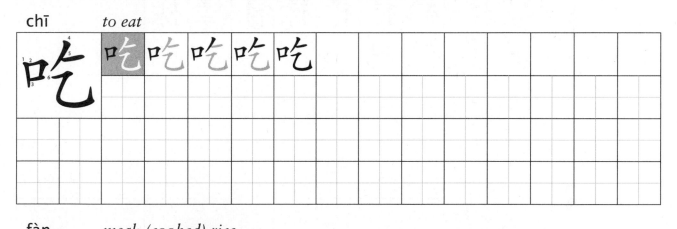

chī   *to eat*

fàn   *meal; (cooked) rice*

zěn *how*

怎

yàng *shape; appearance; manner*

樣 样

tài *too; extremely*

太

le *(particle)*

了

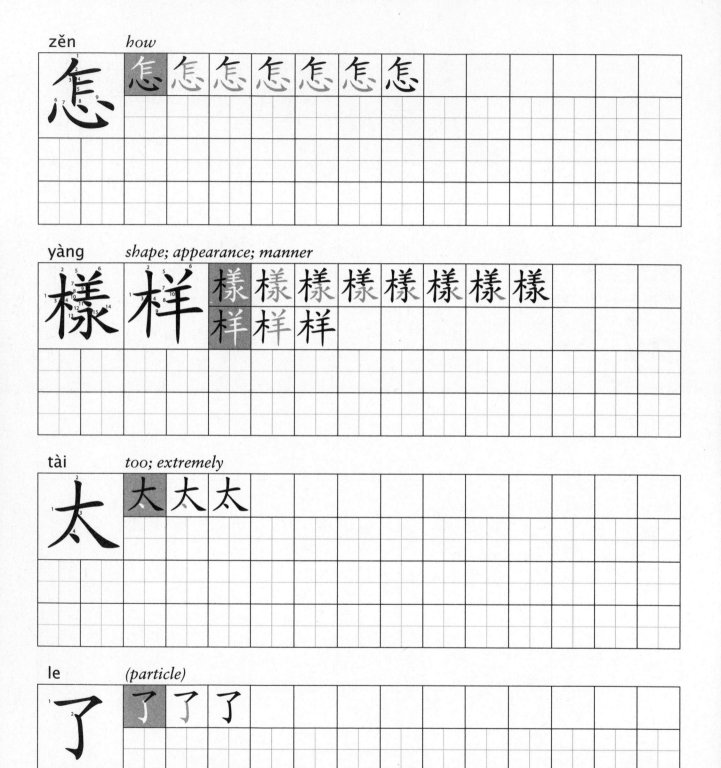

xiè   *to thank*

謝 謝 謝 謝 謝 謝 謝 謝 謝 謝
谢 谢 谢 谢 谢 谢 谢 谢 谢 谢

xǐ   *to like; happy*

喜 喜 喜 喜 喜 喜 喜 喜 喜 喜

huān   *happy; joyous*

歡 歡 歡 歡 歡 歡 歡 歡 歡
欢 欢 欢 欢 欢

cài   *dishes, cuisine*

菜 菜 菜 菜 菜 菜 菜 菜
菜 菜 菜 菜 菜 菜 菜

hái   *still; additionally; alternatively*

還 还

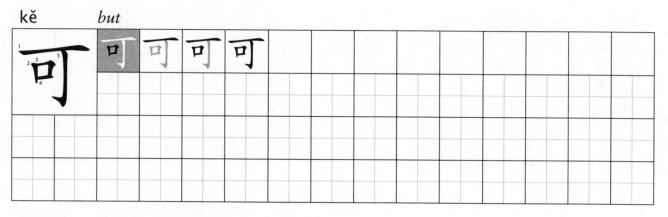

kě   *but*

可

men   *(plural suffix)*

們 们

diǎn *o'clock (lit. dot, point, thus "points on the clock")*

點	点	點	點	點	點	點	點	點	點	點	點
		點	點								
		点	点	点	点	点	点				

bàn *half; half an hour*

| 半 | 半 | 半 | 半 | 半 | 半 | 半 | | | | | |

wǎn *evening; late*

| 晚 | 晚 | 晚 | 晚 | 晚 | 晚 | 晚 | 晚 | 晚 | 晚 | 晚 | |
| | | 晚 | 晚 | 晚 | 晚 | 晚 | 晚 | 晚 | 晚 | 晚 | |

shàng   *above; top*

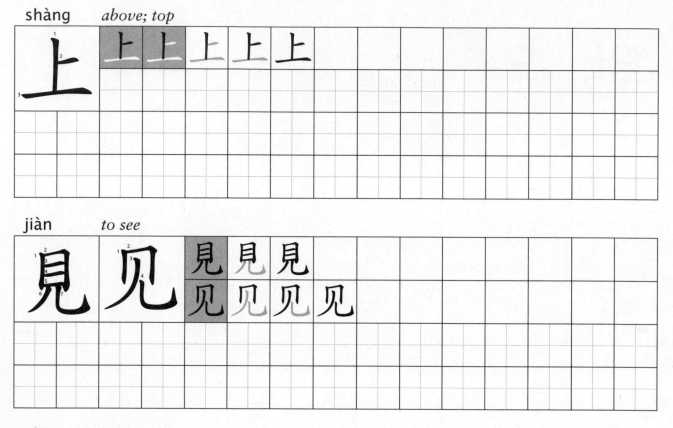

jiàn   *to see*

zài   *again*

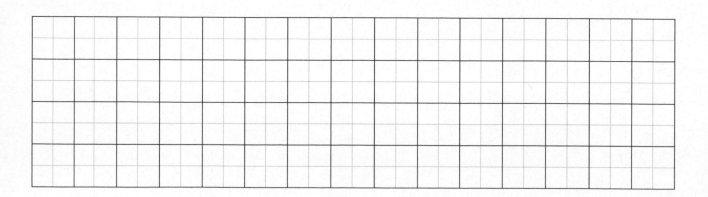

Dialogue II

xiàn   *now*

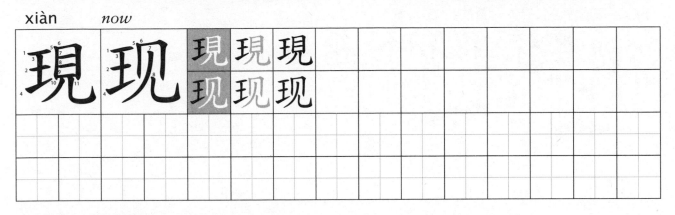

zài   *to be present; at (a place)*

kè   *quarter (of an hour)*

shì   *matter; affair; event*

hěn *very*

很 很 很 很 很 很 很 很

máng *busy*

忙 忙 忙 忙 忙

míng *bright*

明 明 明

wèi *for*

為 為 為 為 為 為 為
为 为 为 为 为

yīn *cause; reason; because*

因　因　因　因　因　因

tóng *same*

同　同　同　同　同　同

rèn *to recognize*

認　认　認　認　認　認　認

认　认　认

shí *to recognize*

識　识　識　識　識　識　識　識

识　识　识　识

Dialogue I

zhōu   *week; cycle*

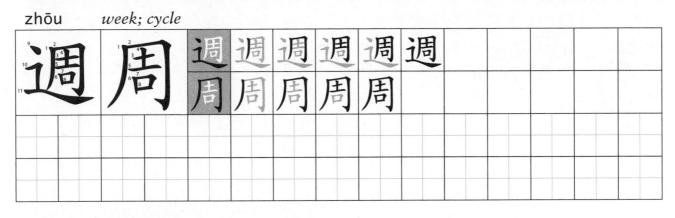

mò   *end*

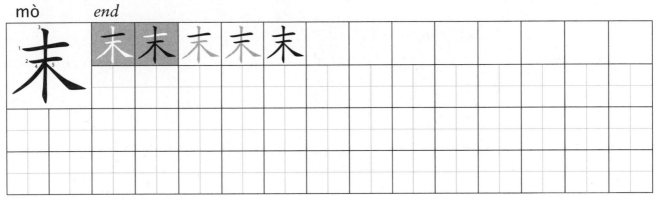

dǎ   *to hit*

qiú   *ball*

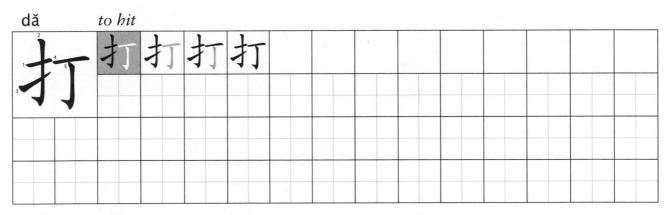

kàn   *to watch; to look; to read*

看　看 看 看 看 看 看 看

diàn   *electricity*

電 电　電 電 電 電
　　　電 电 电 电 电

shì   *vision*

視 视　視 視 視 視
　　　視 视 视 视 视

chàng   *to sing*

唱　唱 唱 唱 唱

gē *song*

歌 歌歌歌

tiào *to jump*

跳 跳跳跳跳跳跳跳

wǔ *to dance; dance*

舞 舞 舞舞舞舞舞舞舞舞舞舞舞
舞

tīng *to listen*

聽 听 聽聽聽聽聽聽聽
听听听听听听

yīn   *sound*

音   音音音

yuè   *music*

樂 乐   樂 樂 樂 樂 樂
         乐 乐 乐 乐

shū   *book*

書 书   書 書 書
         书 书 书 书 书 书

duì   *right; correct*

對 对   對 對 對 對 對 對 對
         对 对 对 对

shí   *time*

時 时 時 時 時 時
时 时 时

hòu   *time; season; await*

候 候 候 候 候 候 候 候

yǐng   *shadow*

影 影 影 影 影 影 影 影

cháng   *often*

常 常 常 常 常 常 常 常

qù   *to go*

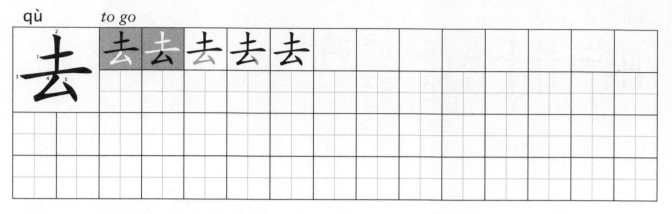

去 去 去 去 去

wài   *outside*

外 外 外 外

kè   *guest*

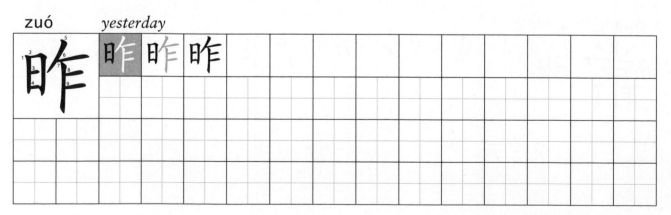

客 客 客 客 客 客

zuó   *yesterday*

昨 昨 昨

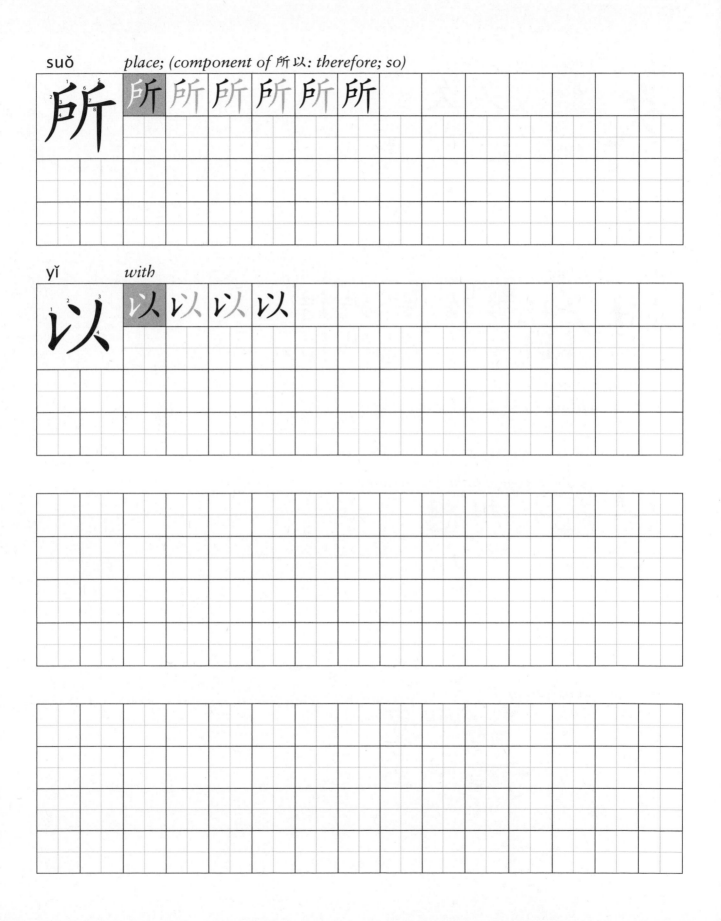

suǒ *place; (component of 所以: therefore; so)*

所

所 所 所 所 所 所

yǐ *with*

以

以 以 以 以

Dialogue II

jiǔ   *long (of time)*

久   久 久 久 久

cuò   *wrong*

錯 错   错 错 错 错 错
              错 错 错 错 错

xiǎng   *to want to; would like to; to think*

想   想 想 想

jué   *to feel; to think*

覺 觉   覺 覺 覺
              觉 觉 觉

de *(particle)*

得 得 得 得 得 得

yì *meaning*

意 意 意 意 意 意

sī *to think*

思 思 思 思 思

zhǐ *only*

只 只 只 只 只

shuì   *to sleep*

睡 睡 睡 睡 睡 睡 睡 睡 睡 睡

suàn   *to calculate*

算 算 算 算 算 算 算 算 算

zhǎo   *to look for*

找 找 找

bié   *other*

别 别 别 别

Dialogue

ya   *(interjectory particle used to soften a question)*

呀   呀 呀 呀 呀 呀 呀

jìn   *to enter*

進 进   進 進 進
进 进 进 进 进

kuài   *fast, quick; quickly*

快   快 快 快 快

lái   *to come*

來 来   來 来 来 来 来 来 来
来 来 来 来 来 来 来

jiè   *to be situated between*

介 介 介 介 介

shào   *to carry on; to continue*

紹 绍 紹 紹 紹 紹
                紹 紹 紹 绍

xià   *below; under*

下 下 下 下 下

xìng   *mood; interest*

興 兴 興 興 興 興 興 興
                兴 兴 兴 兴

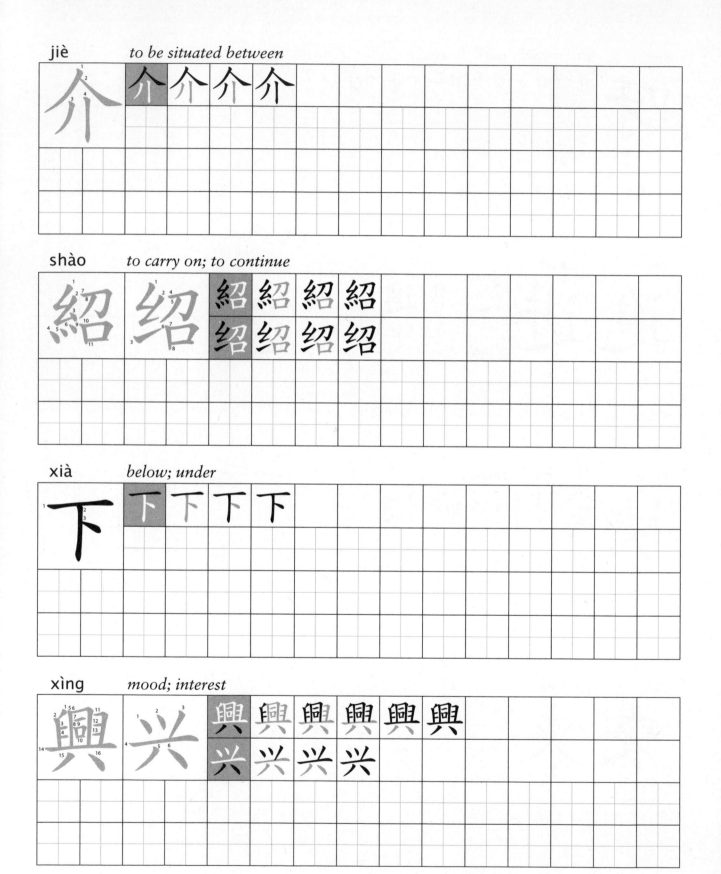

piào   *(component of 漂亮: pretty)*

漂 漂 漂 漂 漂 漂 漂 漂 漂

liàng   *bright*

亮 亮 亮 亮 亮 亮 亮 亮
亮 亮 亮 亮 亮

zuò   *to sit*

坐 坐 坐 坐 坐

nǎ   *where*

哪 哪 哪 哪 哪 哪 哪
哪 哪 哪 哪 哪

xiào *school*

校 校校校校

hē *to drink*

喝 喝喝喝喝喝喝

chá *tea*

茶 茶 茶茶茶茶茶
　　　　茶茶茶茶

kā *(component of* 咖啡: *coffee)*

咖 咖咖咖咖

fēi *(component of 咖啡: coffee)*

ba *(a sentence-final particle)*

yào *to want*

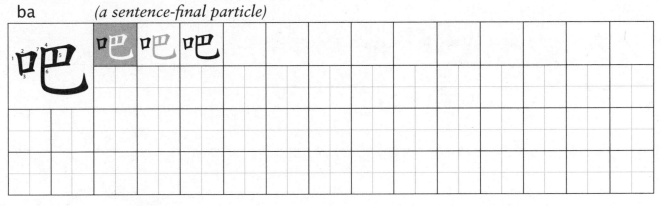

píng *(measure word for bottles); bottle*

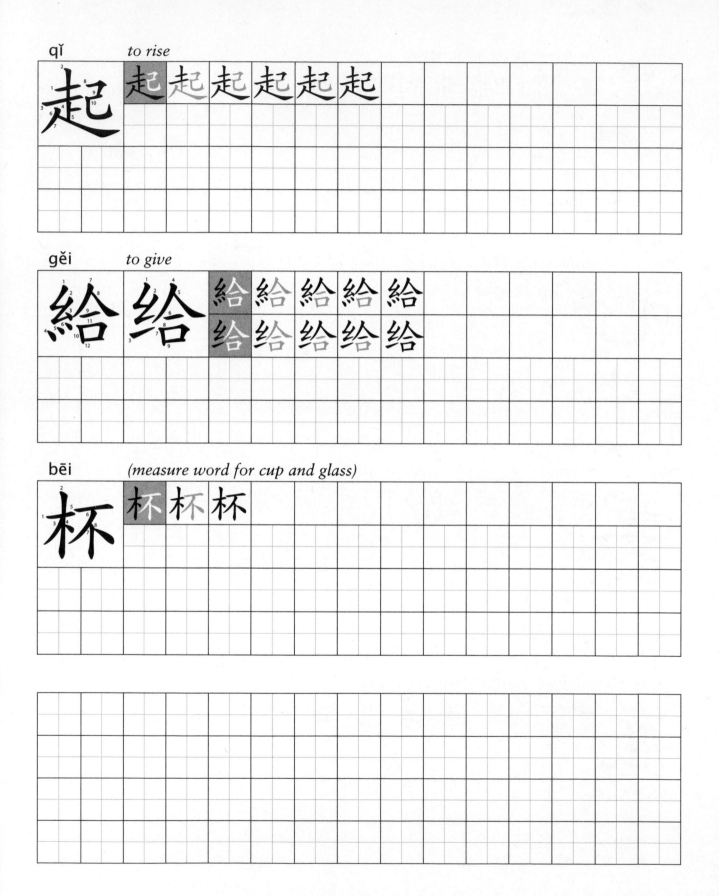

qǐ   *to rise*

gěi   *to give*

bēi   *(measure word for cup and glass)*

Narrative

wán *to have fun; to play*

玩 玩 玩 玩 玩

tú *picture; chart; drawing*

圖 图 图 圖 圖 圖 圖 圖 圖 圖
图 图 图 图 图 图 图

guǎn *place or building (for a service, social, or cultural use)*

館 馆 馆 館 館 館 館 館 館
馆 馆 馆 馆 馆 馆 馆

liáo *to chat*

聊 聊 聊 聊 聊 聊 聊

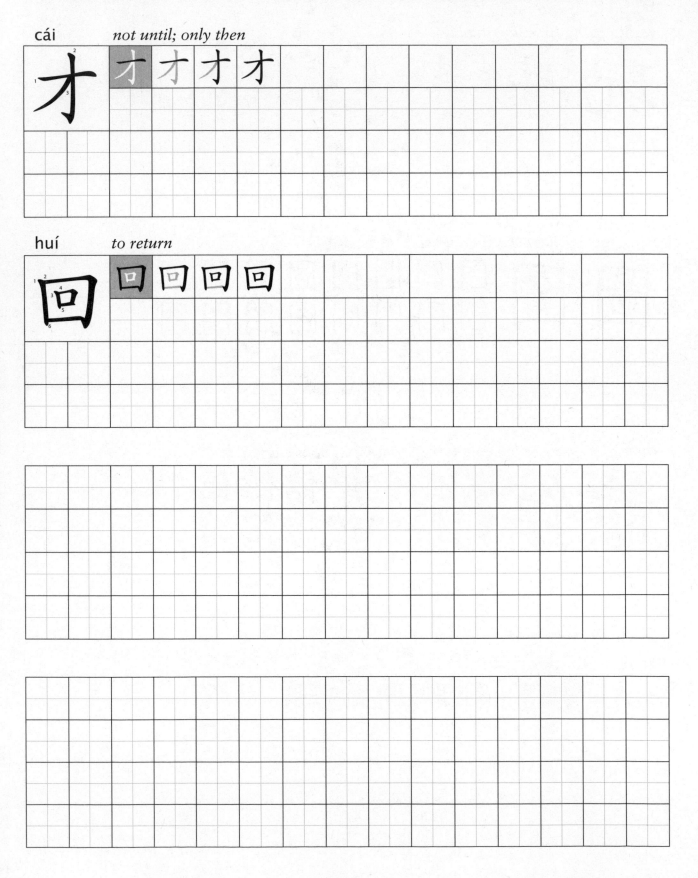

Dialogue I

huà　　*speech*

話　话　話 話 話 話 話
　　　话 话 话 话 话

wéi/wèi　*(on telephone) Hello!; Hey!*

喂　喂 喂 喂 喂 喂 喂

jiù　　*precisely; exactly*

就　就 就 就 就 就 就 就 就 就 就

nín　　*you (honorific for 你)*

您　您 您 您

wèi   *(polite measure word for people)*

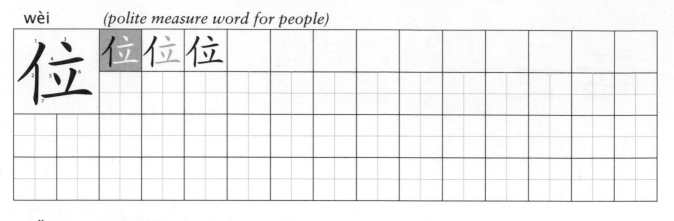

wǔ   *noon*

jiān   *during (a time period); between (two sides)*

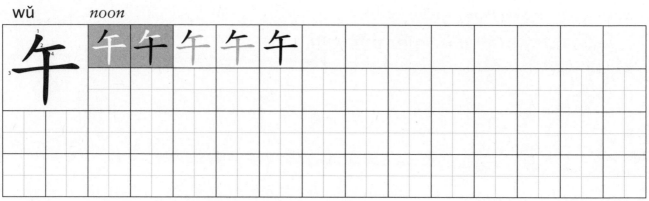

tí   *topic; question*

kāi   *to open; to hold (a meeting, party, etc.)*

開 开 開 開 開
开 开 开

huì   *meeting*

會 会 會 會 會 會 會 會 會 會 會
会 会 会 会 会

jié   *(measure word for class periods)*

節 节 節 節 節 節 節 節 節
节 节 节 节

kè   *class; course; lesson*

課 课 課 課 課 課
课 课 课 课

jí   *level; rank*

级 级 级 级 级 级 级 级
级 级 级 级

kǎo   *to give or take a test*

考 考 考 考 考 考

shì   *test; to try; to experiment*

試 试 試 試 試 試 試 試
试 试 试 试 试 试

hòu   *after; behind; rear*

後 后 後 後 後 後 後
后 后 后 后 后 后

kòng　　*free time*

空　　空 空 空 空 空

fāng　　*square; method*

方　　方 方 方 方 方

biàn　　*convenient; handy*

便　　便 便 便 便 便 便

dào　　*to go to; to arrive*

到　　到 到 到 到 到 到 到

bàn   *to manage*

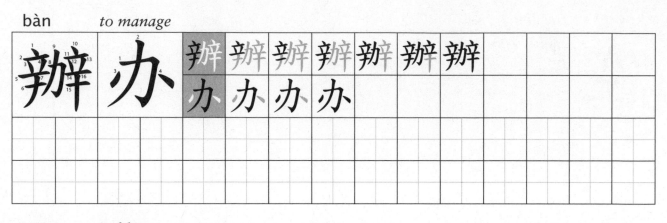

gōng   *public*

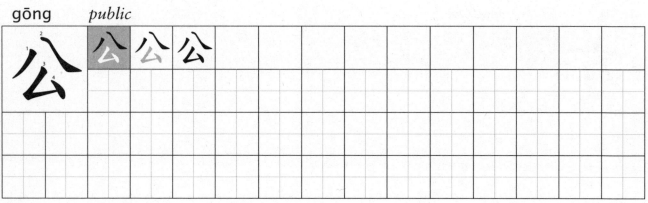

shì   *room*

shì   *room*

xíng   *all right; O.K.*

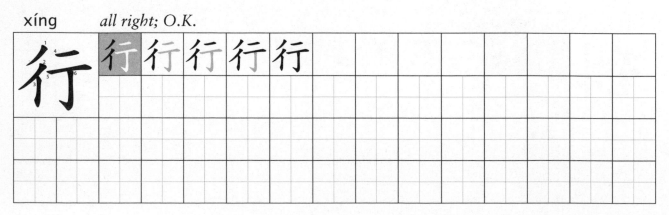

děng *to wait; to wait for*

等 等 等 等 等

qì *air*

氣 气 氣 氣 氣 氣 氣 氣 氣 氣 氣 氣 氣
气 气 气 气 气

Dialogue II

bāng   *to help*

幫   帮

zhǔn   *standard; criterion*

準   准

bèi   *to prepare*

備   备

liàn   *to drill*

練   练

xí *to practice*

習 习   習 習 習 習 習 習 習
         习 习 习 习 习

shuō *to say; to speak*

説 说   说 说 说 说 说 说
         说 说 说 说 说 说

a *(a sentence-final particle of exclamation, interrogation, etc.)*

啊 啊   啊 啊 啊 啊 啊 啊
         啊 啊 啊 啊 啊

dàn *but*

但   但 但 但 但

gēn   *with*

跟　跟　跟　跟

miàn   *face*

面　面　面　面　面　面　面　面　面　面　面

Dialogue I

fù　　　　*to repeat; to duplicate*

xiě　　　　*to write*

màn　　　　*slow*

zhī　　　　*(measure word for long, thin, inflexible objects)*

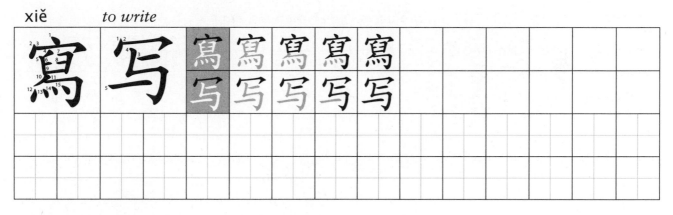

bǐ   *pen*

笔   笔   筆筆筆
           笔笔笔笔

zhāng   *(measure word for flat objects, paper, pictures, etc.)*

張   张   張張張張張張張張张
           张张张张张张

zhǐ   *paper*

紙   纸   紙紙紙紙紙
           纸纸纸纸纸纸

jiāo   *to teach*

教   教教教教教教教

dǒng　*to understand*

懂　懂　懂 懂 懂 懂 懂 懂 懂 懂 懂

zhēn　*true; real(ly)*

真　真 真 真 真 真 真 真 真 真

lǐ　*inside*

裏 里　裏 裏 裏 裏 裏　里 里

yù　*in advance; beforehand*

預 預　預 預 預 預 預 預

dì   *(prefix for ordinal numbers)*

第

yǔ   *language*

語 语

fǎ   *law; rule; method*

法

róng   *to allow; to tolerate*

容

yì   *easy*

易   易 易 易 易 易

cí   *word*

詞 词   詞 詞 詞 詞 詞
          词 词 词 词 词

hàn   *Chinese ethnicity*

漢 汉   漢 漢 漢
          汉 汉 汉

nán   *difficult*

難 难   難 難 難 難 難 難 難 難 難
          难 难 难 难

Dialogue II

píng   *level; even*

平　平 平 平 平 平 平

zǎo   *early*

早　早 早 早 早

gōng   *work; achievement*

功　功 功 功 功

shǐ   *to begin*

始　始 始 始 始

niàn　　*to read aloud*

念　念　念　念

lù　　*to record*

錄　录　錄录　錄录　錄录　錄录　錄录　錄录　錄录

shuài　　*handsome*

帥　帅　帥帅　帥帅　帥帅　帅

kù　　*cool*

酷　酷　酷　酷　酷　酷　酷　酷　酷　酷　酷　酷

Diary

piān　　　*(measure word for essays, articles, etc)*

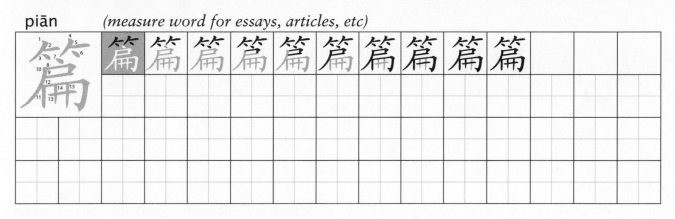

jì　　　*record*

lèi　　　*tired*

累　累　累　累　累

chuáng　　*bed*

床　床　床　床

xǐ   *to wash*

洗　洗洗洗

zǎo   *bath*

澡　澡澡澡澡澡澡

biān   *side*

邊　边　邊邊邊邊邊
　　　　边边边

fā   *to emit; to issue*

發　发　發發發發發發發
　　　　发发发发发发

xīn　*new*

新 新 新 新 新

nǎo　*brain*

腦 脑 腦 腦 腦 腦 腦 腦 腦 腦 腦 腦
脑 脑 脑 脑 脑 脑

cān　*meal*

餐 餐 餐 餐 餐 餐

tīng　*hall*

廳 厅 廳 廳 廳
厅 厅 厅

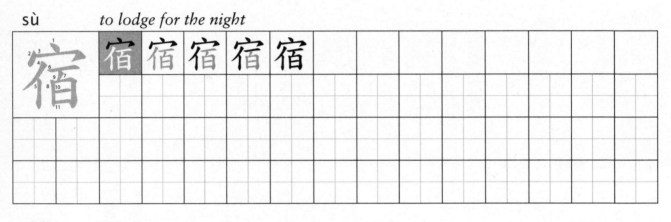

wǎng   *net*

網 网 網 網 網 網 網 網 網 網
       网 网 网 网 网 网

sù   *to lodge for the night*

宿 宿 宿 宿 宿 宿

shè   *house*

舍 舍 舍 舍 舍 舍 舍

zhèng   *just; upright*

正 正 正 正 正 正 正 正

qián   *front; before*

前   前 前 前 前 前 前 前

gào   *to tell; to inform*

告   告 告 告

sù   *to tell; to relate*

訴 诉   诉 诉 诉 诉 诉 诉 诉 诉

yǐ   *already*

已   已 已 已 已

jīng   *to pass through*

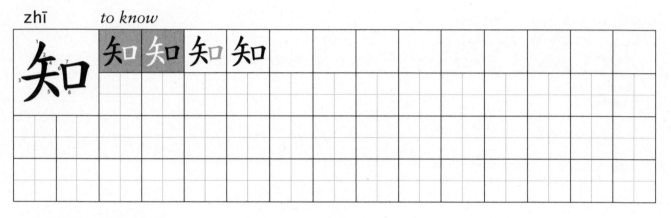

zhī   *to know*

知

dào   *path; way*

道

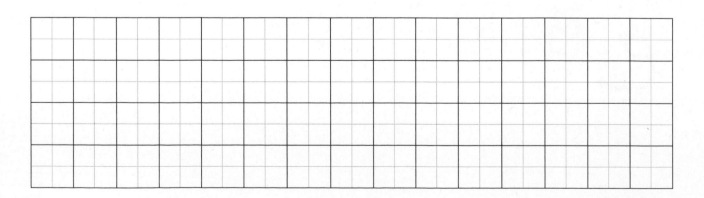

Letter

fēng *(measure word for letters)*

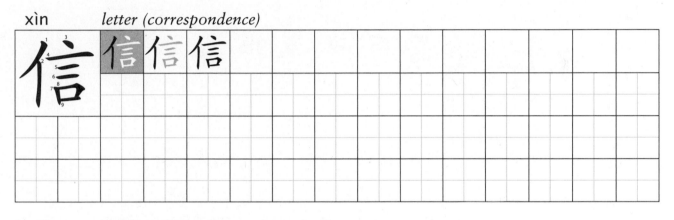

xìn *letter (correspondence)*

zuì *(of superlative degree; most; -est)*

jìn *close; near*

chú   *apart from*

除 除 除除除除除
　　　除除除除除

zhuān   *special*

專 专 專專專專專專
　　　专专专专

yè   *occupation; profession*

業 业 業業業業業業
　　　业业

xī   *to hope; hope*

希   希希希希

wàng　　*to hope; to expect*

望　望 望 望 望 望

néng　　*can; to be able to*

能　能 能 能 能 能 能

yòng　　*to use*

用　用 用 用 用 用

xiào　　*to laugh at; to laugh; to smile*

笑　笑 笑 笑 笑

zhù　　*to wish (well)*

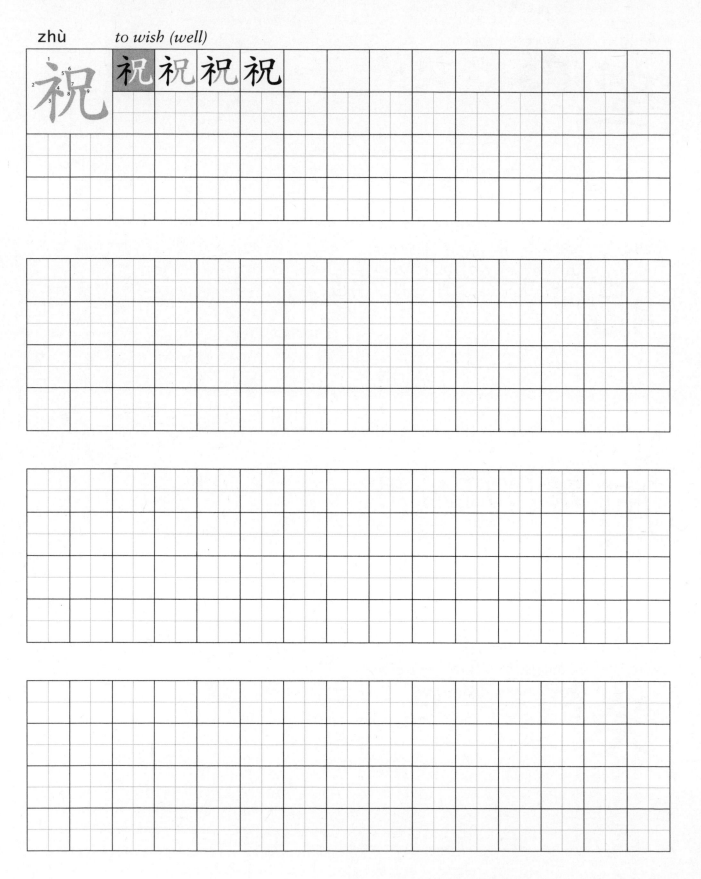

Dialogue I

shāng   *commerce; business*

商 商 商 商 商 商 商 商 商 商 商

diàn   *store; shop*

店 店 店 店 店 店 店 店

mǎi   *to buy*

買 买   買 買 買 買
        买 买 买 买 买 买

dōng   *(component of 東西/东西: things; objects); east*

東 东   東 東 東 東 東
        东 东 东 东

xī   *(component of 東西/东西: things; objects); west*

西   西   西

shòu   *sale; to sell*

售   售 售 售 售

huò   *merchandise*

貨 貨   貨 貨 貨 貨
         货 货 货 货

yuán   *member; personnel*

員 员   員 員 員 員
         员 员 员 员

fú   *clothing*

服   服 服 服

jiàn   *(measure word for shirts, jackets, coats, etc.)*

件   件 件 件 件 件

chèn   *lining*

襯 衬   襯 襯 襯 襯 襯
     衬 衬 衬

shān   *shirt*

衫   衫 衫 衫 衫

yán   *face; countenance*

颜

sè   *color*

色

huáng   *yellow*

黄

hóng   *red*

红

chuān *to wear; to put on*

穿　穿穿穿

tiáo *(measure word for pants and long, thin objects)*

條　条　條條條條條　条条条条条

kù *pants*

褲　褲　褲褲褲褲褲褲褲　裤裤裤裤裤裤裤

yí *suitable; appropriate*

宜　宜宜宜

rú   *as; if*

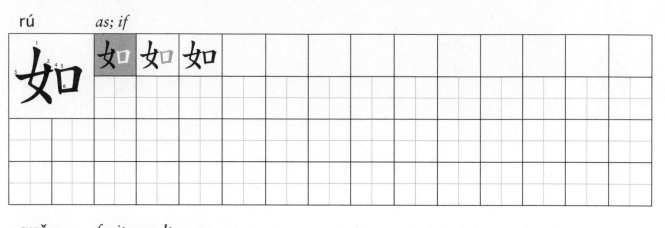

guǒ   *fruit; result*

cháng   *long*

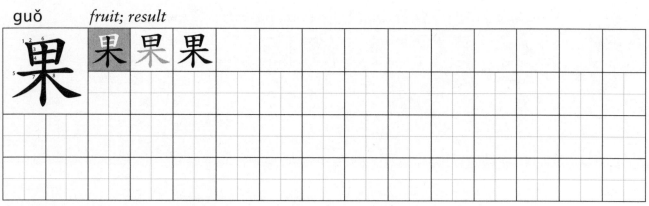

duǎn   *short*

hé *to suit; to fit*

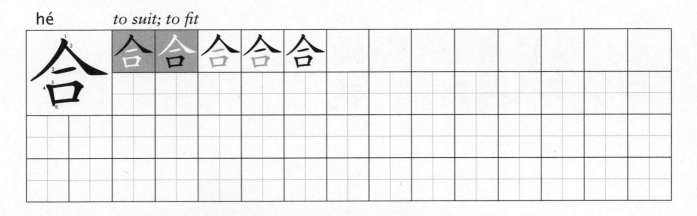

shì *to suit; to be appropriate*

gòng *altogether*

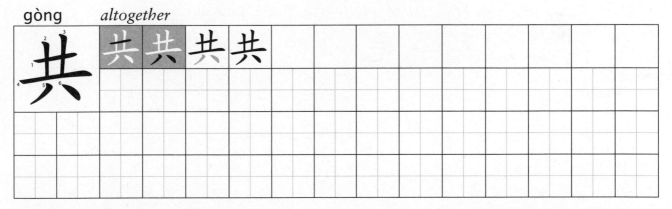

shǎo *few; little; less*

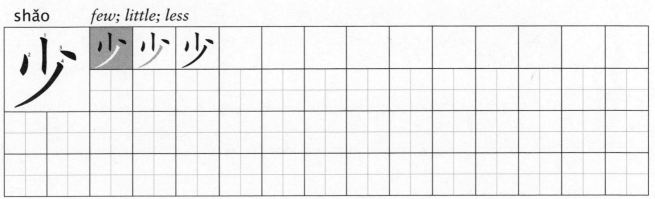

qián money

錢 钱 錢 錢 錢 錢
钱 钱 钱 钱

kuài (measure word for the basic Chinese monetary unit)

塊 块 塊 塊 塊 塊 塊
块 块 块

máo (measure word for 1/10 of a kuai, dime [in US money])

毛 毛 毛 毛 毛 毛

fēn (measure word for 1/100 of a kuai; cent)

分 分 分 分 分

bǎi   *hundred*

百　百百百百

Dialogue II

shuāng *(measure word for a pair)*

雙 | 双 | 雙 雙 雙 雙 雙
双 双 双

xié *shoes*

鞋 | 鞋 鞋 鞋 鞋 鞋 鞋 鞋

huàn *to exchange; to change*

換 | 換 | 換 換 換 換 換 換
換 換 換 換 換

hēi *black*

黑 | 黑 黑 黑

suī   *although*

雖 虽 | 雖 | 雖 | 雖 | 雖 | 雖 | 雖 | 雖
虽 | 虽 | 虽 | 虽 | 虽 | 虽 | 虽

rán   *right; correct; like that*

然   然 然 然 然 然 然 然

zhǒng   *(measure word for kinds, sorts, types)*

種 种 | 種 | 種 | 種 | 種 | 種 | 種 | 種 | 種
种 | 种 | 种 | 种 | 种

tǐng   *very; rather*

挺   挺 挺 挺 挺 挺 挺 挺

tā *it*

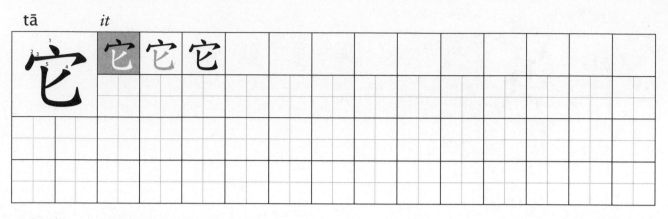

shuā *to brush; to swipe*

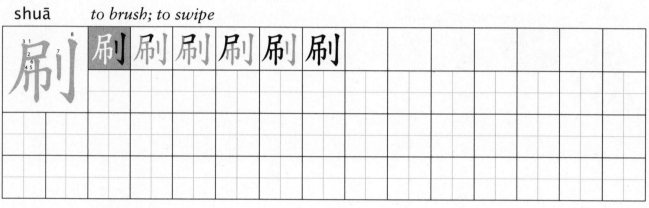

kǎ *card*

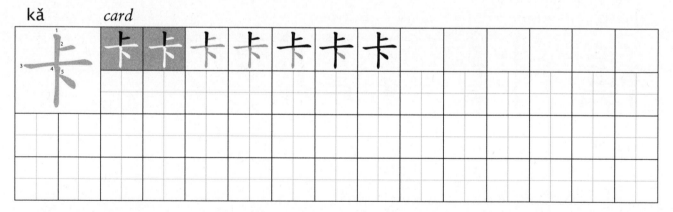

shōu *to receive; to accept*

guò *to pass*

過　过　過過過過過過
　　　过过过

fù *to pay*

付　付付付

Dialogue

hán　　　*cold*

寒　寒 寒 寒 寒 寒 寒 寒 寒

jià　　　*vacation*

假　假 假 假 假 假 假 假 假

fēi　　　*to fly*

jī　　　*machine*

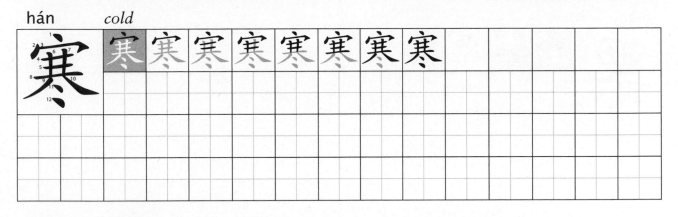

piào   *ticket*

票

chǎng   *field*

場 场

qì   *steam; gas*

汽

chē   *vehicle; car*

車 车

huò   *or*

或   或 或 或 或 或

zhě   *(component of 或者: or)*

者   者 者 者 者 者

dì   *ground; (particle)*

地   地 地 地

tiě   *iron*

鐵 铁   鐵 鐵 鐵 鐵 鐵
    铁 铁 铁 铁

zhàn   *(measure words for stops of bus, train, etc.)*

站　站　站　站

lǜ   *green*

綠　绿　綠　綠　綠
　　　　绿　绿　绿

xiàn   *line; route*

綫　线　綫　綫　綫　綫
　　　　线　线　线

lán   *blue*

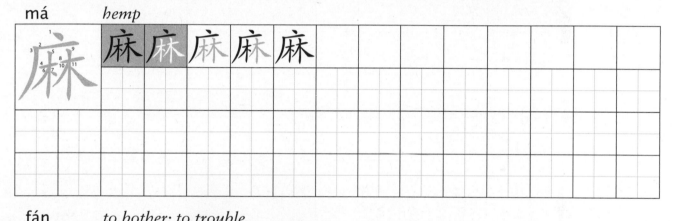

má   *hemp*

fán   *to bother; to trouble*

chū   *to go out*

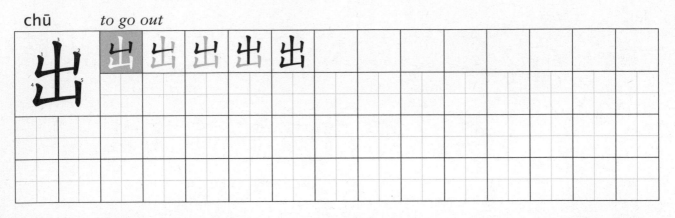

zū   *to rent*

sòng   *to see off or out; to take (someone somewhere)*

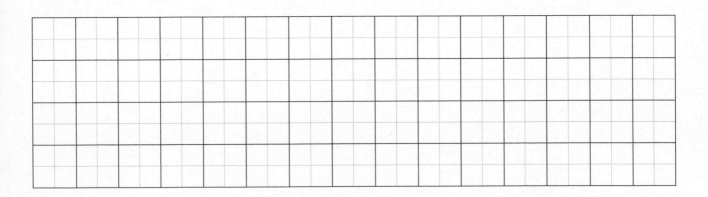

E-mail

yóu   *mail; post*

郵 邮 郵 郵 郵 郵 郵 郵 郵 郵 郵
邮 邮 邮 邮 邮 邮 邮

ràng   *to allow or cause (somebody to do something)*

讓 让 讓 讓 讓 讓 讓 讓 讓
让 让 让

huā   *to spend*

花 花 花 花 花
花 花 花

měi   *every; each*

每 每 每 每 每

chéng   *town*

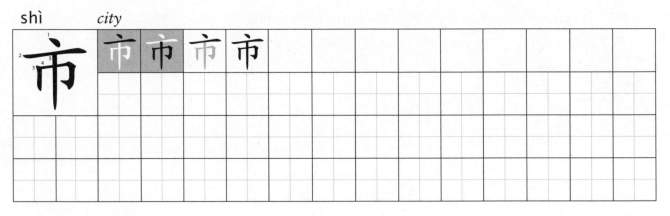

城 城 城 城 城 城 城 城

shì   *city*

市 市 市 市

tè   *special*

特 特 特 特 特 特 特

sù   *speed*

速 速 速 速 速 速 速

jīn   *tense; tight*

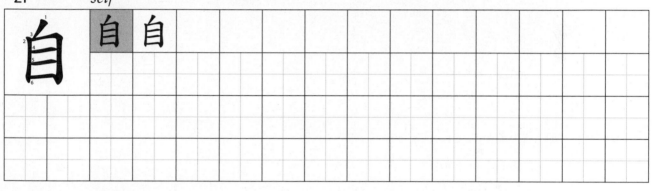

zì   *self*

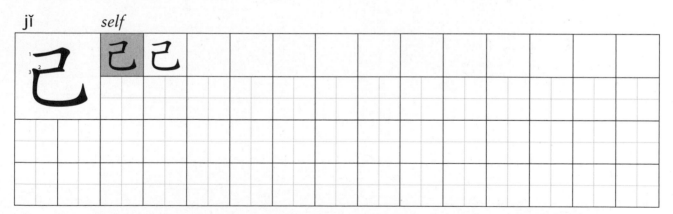

jǐ   *self*

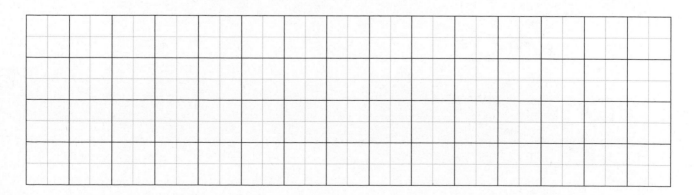

INDEX A
Characters Alphabetically by Pinyin

P = pinyin
T = traditional form
S = simplified form
L = lesson
I = Introduction

Pinyin	Traditional	Simplified	Meaning		
dǒng	懂	懂	to understand	7	79
dōu	都	都	both; all	2	35
duì	對	对	right; correct	4	52
duō	多		many/much; how many/much; to what extent	3	38
ér	兒	儿	son; child	2	30
ěr	耳		ear	1	8
èr	二		two	1	13
fā	發	发	to emit; to issue	8	86
fǎ	法		law; rule; method	7	80
fán	煩	烦	to bother; to trouble	10	113
fàn	飯	饭	meal; (cooked) rice	3	39
fāng	方		square; method	6	71
fēi	飛	飞	to fly	10	109
fēi	啡		(component of 咖啡: coffee)	5	63
fēn	分		(measure word for 1/100 of a kuai, cent)	9	102
fēng	封		(measure word for letters)	8	91
fú	服		clothing	9	97
fù	復	复	to repeat; to duplicate	7	77
fù	付		to pay	9	107
gāo	高		(a surname); tall; high	2	31
gào	告		to tell; to inform	8	89
gē	戈		dagger-axe	1	5
gē	哥		older brother	2	30
gē	歌		song	4	51
gè/ge	個	个	(measure word for many common objects)	2	28
gěi	給	给	to give	5	64
gēn	跟		with	6	76
gōng	工		labor; work	1	4
gōng	弓		bow	1	4
gōng	公		public	6	72
gōng	功		work; achievement	7	82
gòng	共		altogether	9	101
guǎn	館	馆	place or building (for a service, social, or cultural use)	5	65
guì	貴	贵	honorable; expensive	1	18
guó	國	国	country; nation	1	25
guǒ	果		fruit; result	9	100
guò	過	过	to pass	9	107
hái	孩		child	2	29
hái	還	还	still; additionally; alternatively	3	42
hán	寒		cold	10	109
hàn	漢	汉	Chinese ethnicity	7	81
hǎo	好		fine; good; OK; nice; it's settled	1	17
hào	號	号	(measure word for a number in a series; day of the month)	3	37
hē	喝		to drink	5	62
hé	和		and	2	34
hé	合		to suit; to fit	9	101
hēi	黑		black	9	104
hěn	很		very	3	46
hóng	紅	红	red	9	98
hòu	候		time; season; await	4	53
hòu	後	后	after; behind; rear	6	70
huā	花	花	to spend	10	115
huà	話	话	speech	6	67
huān	歡	欢	happy; joyous	3	41
huàn	換	换	to exchange; to change	9	104
huáng	黃		yellow	9	98

huí	回		to return	5	66
huì	會 会		meeting	6	69
huǒ	火		fire	1	6
huò	貨 货		merchandise	9	96
huò	或		or	10	111
jī	機 机		machine	10	109
jí	級 级		level; rank	6	70
jǐ	幾 几		how many; some; a few	2	33
jǐ	己		self	10	117
jì	記 记		record	8	85
jiā	家		family; home	2	33
jià	假		vacation	10	109
jiān	間 间		during (a time period); between (two sides)	6	68
jiàn	見 见		to see	3	44
jiàn	件		(measure word for shirts, jackets, coats, etc.)	9	97
jiāo	教		to teach	7	78
jiào	叫		to be called; to call	1	19
jié	節 节		(measure word for class periods)	6	69
jiě	姐		older sister	1	19
jiè	介		to be situated between	5	60
jīn	金		gold	1	10
jīn	今		today; now	3	38
jǐn	緊 紧		tense; tight	10	117
jìn	進 进		to enter	5	59
jìn	近		close; near	8	91
jīng	京		capital city	1	26
jīng	經 经		to pass through	8	90
jiǔ	九		nine	1	15
jiǔ	久		long (of time)	4	56
jiù	就		precisely; exactly	6	67
jué	覺 觉		to feel; to think	4	56
kā	咖		(component of 咖啡: coffee)	5	62
kǎ	卡		card	9	106
kāi	開 开		to open; to hold (a meeting, party, etc.)	6	69
kàn	看		to watch; to look; to read	4	50
kǎo	考		to give or take a test	6	70
kě	可		but	3	42
kè	刻		quarter (of an hour)	3	45
kè	客		guest	4	54
kè	課 课		class; course; lesson	6	69
kòng	空		free time	6	71
kǒu	口		mouth	1	2
kù	酷		cool	7	83
kù	褲 裤		pants	9	99
kuài	快		fast, quick; quickly	5	59
kuài	塊 块		(measure word for the basic Chinese monetary unit)	9	102
lái	來 来		to come	5	59
lán	藍 蓝		blue	10	113
lǎo	老		old	1	23
le	了		(particle)	3	40
lèi	累		tired	8	85
lǐ	李		(a surname); plum	1	21
lǐ	裏 里		inside	7	79
lì	力		power	1	1
liàn	練 练		to drill	6	74
liǎng	兩 两		two; a couple of	2	33
liàng	亮		bright	5	61
liáo	聊		to chat	5	65
liù	六		six	1	14

lù	錄	录	to record	7	83
lù	律		law; rule	2	34
lù	綠	绿	green	10	112
mā	媽	妈	mother; mom	2	28
má	麻		hemp	10	113
mǎ	馬	马	horse	1	11
ma	嗎	吗	(question particle)	1	23
mǎi	買	买	to buy	9	95
màn	慢		slow	7	77
máng	忙		busy	3	46
máo	毛		(measure word for 1/10 of a kuai, dime [in US money])	9	102
me	麼	么	(question particle)	1	19
méi	没		not	2	31
měi	美		beautiful	1	26
měi	每		every; each	10	115
mèi	妹		younger sister	2	33
mén	門	门	door	1	10
men	們	们	(plural suffix)	3	42
mì	糸		fine silk	1	8
miàn	面		face	6	76
míng	名		name	1	20
míng	明		bright	3	46
mò	末		end	4	49
mù	木		wood	1	6
mù	目		eye	1	7
nǎ	哪	哪	where	5	61
nà	那	那	that	2	27
nán	男		male	2	29
nán	難	难	difficult	7	81
nǎo	腦	脑	brain	8	87
ne	呢		(question particle)	1	18
néng	能		can; to be able to	8	93
nǐ	你		you	1	17

nián	年		year	3	38
niàn	念		to read aloud	7	83
nín	您		you (honorific for 你)	6	67
niǔ	紐	纽	knob; button	1	26
nǚ	女		woman	1	3
péng	朋		friend	1	22
piān	篇		(measure word for articles, etc)	8	85
piàn	片		flat, thin piece	2	27
piào	漂		(component of 漂亮: pretty)	5	61
piào	票		ticket	10	110
píng	瓶		(measure word for bottles); bottle	5	63
píng	平		level; even	7	82
qī	七		seven	1	14
qī	期		period (of time)	3	37
qǐ	起		to rise	5	64
qì	氣	气	air	6	73
qì	汽		steam; gas	10	110
qián	前		front; before	8	89
qián	錢	钱	money	9	102
qǐng	請	请	please (polite form of request); to treat or to invite (somebody)	1	17
qiú	球		ball	4	49
qù	去		to go	4	54
rán	然		right; correct; like that	9	105
ràng	讓	让	to allow or cause (somebody to do something)	10	115
rén	人		person	1	1
rén	人		people; person	1	24
rèn	認	认	to recognize	3	47
rì	日		sun	1	5

Pinyin	Traditional	Simplified	Definition	Lesson	Page
tú	圖	图	picture; chart; drawing	5	65
tǔ	土		earth	1	2
wài	外		outside	4	54
wán	玩		to have fun; to play	5	65
wǎn	晚	晚	evening; late	3	43
wáng	王		(a surname); king	1	21
wǎng	網	网	net	8	88
wàng	望		to hope; to expect	8	93
wéi	口		enclose	1	2
wéi/wèi	喂		(on telephone) Hello!; Hey!	6	67
wèi	為	为	for	3	46
wèi	位		(polite measure word for people)	6	68
wén	文		(written) language; script	2	32
wèn	問	问	to ask (a question)	1	17
wǒ	我		I; me	1	18
wǔ	五		five	1	14
wǔ	舞		to dance; dance	4	51
wǔ	午		noon	6	68
xī	夕		sunset	1	2
xī	希		to hope; hope	8	92
xī	西		(component of 東西/东西: things; objects); west	9	96
xí	習	习	to practice	6	75
xǐ	喜		to like; happy	3	41
xǐ	洗		to wash	8	86
xià	下		below; under	5	60
xiān	先		first	1	20
xiàn	現	现	now	3	45
xiàn	綫	线	line; route	10	112
xiǎng	想		to want to; would like to; to think	4	56
xiǎo	小		small	1	4
xiào	校		school	5	62
xiào	笑		to laugh at; to laugh; to smile	8	93
xié	鞋		shoes	9	104
xiě	寫	写	to write	7	77
xiè	謝	谢	to thank	3	41
xīn	心		heart	1	5
xīn	新		new	8	87
xìn	信		letter (correspondence)	8	91
xīng	星		star	3	37
xíng	行		all right; O.K.	6	72
xìng	姓		(one's) surname is ...; to be surnamed; surname	1	18
xìng	興	兴	mood; interest	5	60
xué	學	学	to study	1	24
ya	呀		(interjectory particle used to soften a question)	5	59
yán	言		speech	1	9
yán	顏	颜	face; countenance	9	98
yàng	樣	样	shape; appearance; manner	3	40
yāo	幺		tiny; small	1	4
yào	要		to want	5	63
yě	也		too; also	1	24
yè	業	业	occupation; profession	8	92
yī	衣		clothing	1	8
yī	一		one	1	13
yī	醫	医	doctor; medicine	2	35
yí	宜		suitable; appropriate	9	99

yǐ	已		already	8	89
yǐ	以		with	4	55
yì	意		meaning	4	57
yì	易		easy	7	81
yīn	因		cause; reason; because	3	47
yīn	音		sound	4	52
yīng	英	英	flower; hero; England	2	36
yǐng	影		shadow	4	53
yòng	用		to use	8	93
yóu	郵	邮	mail; post	10	115
yǒu	友		friend	1	21
yǒu	有		to have; to exist	2	31
yòu	又		right hand; again	1	1
yǔ	雨		rain	1	11
yǔ	語	语	language	7	80
yù	預	预	in advance; beforehand	7	79
yuán	員	员	member; personnel	9	96
yuē	約	约	agreement; appointment	1	26
yuè	月		moon	1	6
yuè	樂	乐	music	4	52
zài	再		again	3	44
zài	在		to be present; at (a place)	3	45
zǎo	早		early	7	82
zǎo	澡		bath	8	86
zěn	怎		how	3	40
zhàn	站		(measure words for stops of bus, train, etc.)	10	112
zhāng	張	张	(measure word for flat objects, paper, pictures, etc.)	7	78
zhǎo	找		to look for	4	58
zhào	照		photograph; to illuminate; to shine	2	27
zhě	者		(component of 或者: or)	10	111
zhè	這	这	this	2	28
zhēn	真		true; real(ly)	7	79
zhèng	正		just; upright	8	88
zhī	枝		(measure word for long, thin, inflexible objects)	7	77
zhī	知		to know	8	90
zhǐ	只		only	4	57
zhǐ	紙	纸	paper	7	78
zhōng	中		center; middle	1	25
zhǒng	種	种	(measure word for kinds, sorts, types)	9	105
zhōu	週	周	week; cycle	4	49
zhù	祝		to wish (well)	8	94
zhuān	專	专	special	8	92
zhuī	隹		short-tailed bird	1	10
zhǔn	準	准	standard; criterion	6	74
zǐ	子		son	1	3
zì	字		character	1	20
zì	自		self	10	117
zǒu	走		walk	1	9
zū	租		to rent	10	114
zú	足		foot	1	9
zuì	最		(of superlative degree; most; -est)	8	91
zuó	昨		yesterday	4	54
zuò	作		to work; to do	2	34
zuò	做		to do	2	34
zuò	坐		to sit	5	61

INDEX B
Characters by Lesson and Pinyin

P = pinyin
T = traditional form
S = simplified form
L = lesson
I = Introduction

P	T	S	Definition	L	Page
bā	八		eight	I	14
bèi	貝	贝	cowrie shell	I	9
cùn	寸		inch	I	3
dà	大		big	I	3
dāo	刀		knife	I	1
ěr	耳		ear	I	8
èr	二		two	I	13
gē	戈		dagger-axe	I	5
gōng	工		labor; work	I	4
gōng	弓		bow	I	4
huǒ	火		fire	I	6
jīn	金		gold	I	10
jiǔ	九		nine	I	15
kǒu	口		mouth	I	2
lì	力		power	I	1
liù	六		six	I	14
mǎ	馬	马	horse	I	11
mén	門	门	door	I	10
mì	糸		fine silk	I	8
mù	木		wood	I	6
mù	目		eye	I	7
nǚ	女		woman	I	3
qī	七		seven	I	14
rén	人		person	I	1
rì	日		sun	I	5
sān	三		three	I	13
shí	食		eat	I	11
shí	十		ten	I	15
shì	示		show	I	7
shǒu	手		hand	I	5
shuǐ	水		water	I	6
sì	四		four	I	13
tián	田		field	I	7
tǔ	土		earth	I	2
wéi	囗		enclose	I	2
wǔ	五		five	I	14
xī	夕		sunset	I	2
xiǎo	小		small	I	4
xīn	心		heart	I	5
yán	言		speech	I	9
yāo	幺		tiny; small	I	4
yī	衣		clothing	I	8
yī	一		one	I	13
yòu	又		right hand; again	I	1
yǔ	雨		rain	I	11
yuè	月		moon	I	6
zhuī	隹		short-tailed bird	I	10
zǐ	子		son	I	3
zǒu	走		walk	I	9
zú	足		foot	I	9
běi	北		north	1	25
bù	不		not; no	1	24
guì	貴	贵	honorable; expensive	1	18
guó	國	国	country; nation	1	25
hǎo	好		fine; good; OK; nice; it's settled	1	17
jiào	叫		to be called; to call	1	19
jiě	姐		older sister	1	19
jīng	京		capital city	1	26
lǎo	老		old	1	23
lǐ	李		(a surname); plum	1	21

Pinyin	Traditional	Simplified	Meaning		
ma	嗎	吗	(question particle)	1	23
měi	美		beautiful	1	26
míng	名		name	1	20
me	麼	么	(question particle)	1	19
ne	呢		(question particle)	1	18
nǐ	你		you	1	17
niǔ	紐	纽	knob; button	1	26
péng	朋		friend	1	22
qǐng	請	请	please (polite form of request); to treat or to invite (somebody)	1	17
rén	人		people; person	1	24
shén	什		what	1	19
shēng	生		birth; to be born	1	20
shī	師	师	teacher	1	23
shì	是		to be	1	23
wáng	王		(a surname); king	1	21
wèn	問	问	to ask (a question)	1	17
wǒ	我		I; me	1	18
xiān	先		first	1	20
xìng	姓		(one's) surname is ...; to be surnamed; surname	1	18
xué	學	学	to study	1	24
yě	也		too; also	1	24
yǒu	友		friend	1	21
yuē	約	约	agreement; appointment	1	26
zhōng	中		center; middle	1	25
zì	字		character	1	20
ài	愛	爱	love; to love	2	36
bà	爸		father; dad	2	28
bái	白		(a surname); white	2	35
de	的		(a possessive or descriptive particle)	2	27
dì	弟		younger brother	2	30
dōu	都	都	both; all	2	35
ér	兒	儿	son; child	2	30
gāo	高		(a surname); tall; high	2	31
gē	哥		older brother	2	30
gè/ge	個	个	(measure word for many common objects)	2	28
hái	孩		child	2	29
hé	和		and	2	34
jǐ	幾	几	how many; some; a few	2	33
jiā	家		family; home	2	33
liǎng	兩	两	two; a couple of	2	33
lù	律		law; rule	2	34
mā	媽	妈	mother; mom	2	28
méi	沒		not	2	31
mèi	妹		younger sister	2	33
nà	那	那	that	2	27
nán	男		male	2	29
piàn	片		flat, thin piece	2	27
shéi	誰	谁	who	2	29
tā	她		she; her	2	29
tā	他		he; him	2	30
wén	文		(written) language; script	2	32
yī	醫	医	doctor; medicine	2	35
yīng	英	英	flower; hero; England	2	36
yǒu	有		to have; to exist	2	31
zhào	照		photograph; to illuminate; to shine	2	27
zhè	這	这	this	2	28
zuò	作		to work; to do	2	34
zuò	做		to do	2	34

Pinyin	Trad.	Simp.	Meaning		
bàn	半		half; half an hour	3	43
cài	菜	菜	dishes, cuisine	3	41
chī	吃		to eat	3	39
diǎn	點	点	o'clock (lit. dot, point, thus "points on the clock")	3	43
duō	多		many/much; how many/much; to what extent3		38
fàn	飯	饭	meal; (cooked) rice	3	39
hái	還	还	still; additionally; alternatively	3	42
hào	號	号	(measure word for a number in a series; day of the month)	3	37
hěn	很		very	3	46
huān	歡	欢	happy; joyous	3	41
jiàn	見	见	to see	3	44
jīn	今		today; now	3	38
kě	可		but	3	42
kè	刻		quarter (of an hour)	3	45
le	了		(particle)	3	40
máng	忙		busy	3	46
men	們	们	(plural suffix)	3	42
míng	明		bright	3	46
nián	年		year	3	38
qī	期		period (of time)	3	37
rèn	認	认	to recognize	3	47
shàng	上		above; top	3	44
shí	識	识	to recognize	3	47
shì	事		matter; affair; event	3	45
suì	歲	岁	year (of age)	3	39
tài	太		too; extremely	3	40
tiān	天		day	3	37
tóng	同		same	3	47
wǎn	晚	晚	evening; late	3	43
wèi	為	为	for	3	46
xǐ	喜		to like; happy	3	41
xiàn	現	现	now	3	45
xiè	謝	谢	to thank	3	41
xīng	星		star	3	37
yàng	樣	样	form; kind	3	40
yīn	因		cause; reason; because	3	47
zài	再		again	3	44
zài	在		to be present; at (a place)	3	45
zěn	怎		how	3	40
bié	別		other	4	58
cháng	常		often	4	53
chàng	唱		to sing	4	50
cuò	錯	错	wrong	4	56
dǎ	打		to hit	4	49
de	得		(particle)	4	57
diàn	電	电	electricity	4	50
duì	對	对	right; correct	4	52
gē	歌		song	4	51
hòu	候		time; season; await	4	53
jiǔ	久		long (of time)	4	56
jué	覺	觉	to feel; to think	4	56
kàn	看		to watch; to look; to read	4	50
kè	客		guest	4	54
mò	末		end	4	49
qiú	球		ball	4	49
qù	去		to go	4	54
shí	時	时	time	4	53
shì	視	视	vision	4	50
shū	書	书	book	4	52
shuì	睡		to sleep	4	58
sī	思		to think	4	57

suàn	算		to calculate	4	58
suǒ	所		place; (component of 所以: therefore; so)	4	55
tiào	跳		to jump	4	51
tīng	聽	听	to listen	4	51
wài	外		outside	4	54
wǔ	舞		to dance; dance	4	51
xiǎng	想		to want to; would like to; to think	4	56
yǐ	以		with	4	55
yì	意		meaning	4	57
yīn	音		sound	4	52
yǐng	影		shadow	4	53
yuè	樂	乐	music	4	52
zhǎo	找		to look for	4	58
zhǐ	只		only	4	57
zhōu	週	周	week; cycle	4	49
zuó	昨		yesterday	4	54
ba	吧		(a sentence-final particle)	5	63
bēi	杯		(measure word for cup and glass)	5	64
cái	才		not until; only then	5	66
chá	茶	茶	tea	5	62
fēi	啡		(component of 咖啡: coffee)	5	63
gěi	給	给	to give	5	64
guǎn	館	馆	place or building (for a service, social, or cultural use)	5	65
hē	喝		to drink	5	62
huí	回		to return	5	66
jiè	介		to be situated between	5	60
jìn	進	进	to enter	5	59
kā	咖		(component of 咖啡: coffee)	5	62
kuài	快		fast, quick; quickly	5	59
lái	來	来	to come	5	59
liàng	亮	亮	bright	5	61
liáo	聊		to chat	5	65
nǎ	哪	哪	where	5	61
piào	漂		(component of 漂亮: pretty)	5	61
píng	瓶		(measure word for bottles); bottle	5	63
qǐ	起		to rise	5	64
shào	紹	绍	to carry on; to continue	5	60
tú	圖	图	picture; chart; drawing	5	65
wán	玩		to have fun; to play	5	65
xià	下		below; under	5	60
xiào	校		school	5	62
xìng	興	兴	mood; interest	5	60
ya	呀		(interjectory particle used to soften a question)	5	59
yào	要		to want	5	63
zuò	坐		to sit	5	61
a	啊	啊	(a sentence-final particle of exclamation, interrogation, etc.)	6	75
bàn	辦	办	to manage	6	72
bāng	幫	帮	to help	6	74
bèi	備	备	to prepare	6	74
biàn	便		convenient; handy	6	71
dàn	但		but	6	75
dào	到		to go to; to arrive	6	71
děng	等		to wait; to wait for	6	73

fāng	方		square; method	6 71
gēn	跟		with	6 76
gōng	公		public	6 72
hòu	後	后	after; behind; rear	6 71
huà	話	话	speech	6 67
huì	會	会	meeting	6 69
jí	級	级	level; rank	6 70
jiān	間	间	during (a time period); between (two sides)	6 68
jié	節	节	(measure word for class periods)	6 69
jiù	就		precisely; exactly	6 67
kāi	開	开	to open; to hold (a meeting, party, etc.)	6 69
kǎo	考		to give or take a test	6 70
kè	課	课	class; course; lesson	6 69
kòng	空		free time	6 71
liàn	練	练	to drill	6 74
miàn	面		face	6 76
nín	您		you (honorific for 你)	6 67
qì	氣	气	air	6 73
shì	室		room	6 72
shì	試	试	test; to try; to experiment	6 70
shuō	説	说	to say; to speak	6 75
tí	題	题	topic; question	6 68
wéi/wèi	喂		(on telephone) Hello!; Hey!	6 67
wèi	位		(polite measure word for people)	6 68
wǔ	午		noon	6 68
xí	習	习	to practice	6 75
xíng	行		all right; O.K.	6 72
zhǔn	準	准	standard; criterion	6 74
bǐ	筆	笔	pen	7 78
cí	詞	词	word	7 81
dì	第		(prefix for ordinal numbers)	7 80
dǒng	懂	懂	to understand	7 79
fǎ	法		law; rule; method	7 80
fù	復	复	to repeat; to duplicate	7 77
gōng	功		work; achievement	7 82
hàn	漢	汉	Chinese ethnicity	7 81
jiāo	教		to teach	7 78
kù	酷		cool	7 83
lǐ	裏	里	inside	7 79
lù	錄	录	to record	7 83
màn	慢		slow	7 77
nán	難	难	difficult	7 81
niàn	念		to read aloud	7 83
píng	平		level; even	7 82
róng	容		to allow; to tolerate	7 80
shǐ	始		to begin	7 82
shuài	帥	帅	handsome	7 84
xiě	寫	写	to write	7 77
yì	易		easy	7 81
yǔ	語	语	language	7 80
yù	預	预	in advance; beforehand	7 79
zǎo	早		early	7 82
zhāng	張	张	(measure word for flat objects, paper, pictures, etc.)	7 78
zhēn	真		true; real(ly)	7 79
zhī	枝		(measure word for long, thin, inflexible objects)	7 77
zhǐ	紙	纸	paper	7 78
biān	邊	边	side	8 86

cān	餐		meal	8	87
chú	除	除	apart from	8	92
chuáng	床		bed	8	85
dào	道		path; way	8	90
fā	發	发	to emit; to issue	8	86
fēng	封		(measure word for letters)	8	91
gào	告		to tell; to inform	8	89
jì	記	记	record	8	85
jìn	近		close; near	8	91
jīng	經	经	to pass through	8	90
lèi	累		tired	8	85
nǎo	腦	脑	brain	8	87
néng	能		can; to be able to	8	93
piān	篇		(measure word for essays, articles, etc)	8	85
qián	前		front; before	8	89
shè	舍		house	8	88
sù	宿		to lodge for the night	8	88
sù	訴	诉	to tell; to relate	8	89
tīng	廳	厅	hall	8	87
wǎng	網	网	net	8	88
wàng	望		to hope; to expect	8	93
xī	希		to hope; hope	8	92
xǐ	洗		to wash	8	86
xiào	笑		to laugh at; to laugh; to smile	8	93
xīn	新		new	8	87
xìn	信		letter (correspondence)	8	91
yè	業	业	occupation; profession	8	92
yǐ	已		already	8	89
yòng	用		to use	8	88
zǎo	澡		bath	8	86
zhèng	正		just; upright	8	90
zhī	知		to know	8	90
zhù	祝		to wish (well)	8	94
zhuān	專	专	special	8	92
zuì	最		(of superlative degree; most; –est)	8	91
bǎi	百		hundred	9	103
cháng	長	长	long	9	100
chèn	襯	衬	lining	9	97
chuān	穿		to wear; to put on	9	99
diàn	店		store; shop	9	95
dōng	東	东	(component of 東西/东西: things; objects); east	9	95
fēn	分		(measure word for 1/100 of a kuai, cent)	9	102
fú	服		clothing	9	97
fù	付		to pay	9	107
gòng	共		altogether	9	101
guǒ	果		fruit; result	9	100
guò	過	过	to pass	9	107
hé	合		to suit; to fit	9	101
hēi	黑		black	9	104
hóng	紅	红	red	9	98
huàn	換	换	to exchange; to change	9	104
huáng	黃		yellow	9	98
huò	貨	货	merchandise	9	96
jiàn	件		(measure word for shirts, jackets, coats, etc.)	9	97
kǎ	卡		card	9	106
kù	褲	裤	pants	9	99
kuài	塊	块	(measure word for the basic Chinese monetary unit)	9	102

mǎi	買	买	to buy	9	95
máo	毛		(measure word for 1/10 of a kuai, dime [in US money])	9	102
qián	錢	钱	money	9	102
rán	然		right; correct; like that	9	105
sè	色		color	9	98
shān	衫		shirt	9	97
shāng	商		commerce; business	9	95
shǎo	少		few; little; less	9	101
shì	適	适	to suit; to be appropriate	9	101
shōu	收		to receive; to accept	9	106
shòu	售		sale; to sell	9	96
shuā	刷		to brush; to swipe	9	106
shuāng	雙	双	(measure word for a pair)	9	104
suī	雖	虽	although	9	105
tā	它		it	9	106
tiáo	條	条	(measure word for pants and long, thin objects)	9	99
tǐng	挺		very; rather	9	105
xī	西		(component of 東西/东西: things; objects); west	9	96
xié	鞋		shoes	9	104
yán	顏	颜	face; countenance	9	98
yí	宜		suitable; appropriate	9	99
yuán	員	员	member; personnel	9	96
zhǒng	種	种	(measure word for kinds, sorts, types)	9	105
chǎng	場	场	field	10	110
chē	車	车	vehicle; car	10	110
chéng	城		town	10	116

chū	出		to go out	10	114
dì	地		ground; (particle)	10	111
fán	煩	烦	to bother; to trouble	10	113
fēi	飛	飞	to fly	10	109
hán	寒		cold	10	109
huā	花	花	to spend	10	115
huò	或		or	10	111
jī	機	机	machine	10	109
jǐ	己		self	10	117
jià	假		vacation	10	109
jǐn	緊	紧	tense; tight	10	117
lán	藍	蓝	blue	10	113
lǜ	綠	绿	green	10	112
má	麻		hemp	10	113
měi	每		every; each	10	115
piào	票		ticket	10	110
qì	汽		steam; gas	10	110
ràng	讓	让	to allow or cause (somebody to do something)	10	115
shì	市		city	10	118
sòng	送		to see off or out; to take (someone somewhere)	10	114
sù	速		speed	10	118
tè	特		special	10	116
tiě	鐵	铁	iron	10	111
xiàn	綫	线	line; route	10	112
yóu	郵	邮	mail; post	10	115
zhàn	站		(measure words for stops of bus, train, etc.)	10	112
zhě	者		(component of 或者: or)	10	111
zì	自		self	10	117
zū	租		to rent	10	114

Expand your *Integrated Chinese* Study
with support for the whole series

Textbooks, Workbooks, Character Workbooks, Teacher's Handbooks, and **Audio CDs** *work together as a comprehensive curriculum.*

Online Workbooks, eTextbooks, BuilderCards, *and* **Textbook DVDs for all levels** *take study further and add flexibility to the classroom.*

INTEGRATED CHINESE COMPANION WEBSITE
More supplements for students, more support for teachers!

www.cheng-tsui.com/integratedchinese

Kù Chinese

eFlashcards

STUDENTS Sharpen your vocabulary recognition and pronunciation with new *eFlashcards* and learn fun idioms and slang with the video series *Kù Chinese.*

TEACHERS Enhance your classroom instruction with *Video Activity Worksheets* (available for all *Integrated Chinese* DVDs), sentence pattern drills, teacher-generated PowerPoints®, and additional tools for testing and assessment.

Visit **www.cheng-tsui.com** or call 1-800-554-1963 for more information about other supplementary materials, such as graded readers, listening comprehension workbooks, character guides, and reference materials.